Preparing for Worship

SUNDAYS AND FEAST DAYS— CYCLE B

Daniel Donovan

PAULIST PRESS
New York/Mahwah

Library of Congress Cataloging-in-Publication Data

Donovan, Daniel, 1937–
Preparing for worship: Sundays and feast days/Daniel
Donovan.
    p.   cm.
Contents: –[2] Cycle B.
ISBN 0-8091-3424-1
1. Church year meditations. 2./ Bible–Liturgical lessons,
English. I. Title.
BX2170.C55D625   1993
242'.3–dc20   93-13704
                                                CIP

Published by Paulist Press
997 Macarthur Boulevard
Mahwah, New Jersey 07430

Printed and bound in the United States of America

Contents

Introduction 1

1. Advent 5

2. The Christmas Season 19

3. Ordinary Time: Sundays 2 to 8 39

4. Lent 63

5. Easter and the Easter Season 83

6. Trinity Sunday and Corpus Christi....................................113

7. Ordinary Time: Sundays 9 to 34 121

8. Assumption, All Saints, and Immaculate Conception 201

FOR NOREEN AND CATHERINE

Faithful friends are a secure shelter;
Whoever finds one has found a treasure.
                              —*The Wisdom of Sirach*

Introduction

Vatican II has reminded us how central the scriptures are meant to be to our individual and collective efforts to develop a life of genuine Christian discipleship. The liturgical renewal fostered by the council has put a particular emphasis on the role that scriptural readings are to play in the eucharist as, indeed, in the celebration of all the sacraments. Word and sacrament belong together and mutually condition and deepen each other's fruitfulness.

The council was anxious that the Catholic community be exposed to a wider range of scriptural texts than in the past. This resulted in the post-conciliar period in the development of the present three-year cycle of readings, ordinarily referred to by the first three letters of the alphabet. The major distinguishing feature among the three years is the gospel that is read on the so-called Sundays of ordinary time. Matthew, Mark and Luke are used in cycles A, B, and C, respectively. Because Mark is much the shortest of the three, it is supplemented at one point by the reading of the discourse on the bread of life from chapter 6 of John. The present book, the first of three projected volumes, is made up of a series of reflections focused on cycle B.

Sundays and feast days have three readings, the first of which is ordinarily taken from the Old Testament. It is almost always chosen because of some more or less obvious relationship to the gospel of the day. The second reading, usually from Paul or from one of the other writers of New Testament letters, tends to be independent of the gospel. The wide range of texts used here reflects a desire to make available during the course of the three-year period as much of the New Testament as possible.

The liturgical year is built around two fundamental feasts, Easter and Christmas. The older and liturgically more significant of the two focuses on the saving event of Jesus' death and resurrection. Called the paschal mystery or the Christian Passover, it

1

was seen from the beginning to be the heart of both the new faith and its ritual. Rendered present in its power for reconciliation and renewal in the eucharist, it is the focus of every Sunday's liturgy as well as of the yearly solemn celebration of the Easter triduum.

Developed later as a distinctive feast, Christmas recalls both the historical event of the birth of Jesus and the mystery of his person. The incarnation and the paschal mystery are the two major poles of our understanding of the person and work of Jesus as well as of our liturgical celebration of them.

In analogous ways both Easter and Christmas became the centers of major divisions of the church year. Both are preceded by periods of preparation, known respectively as Lent and Advent, and both are prolonged over a series of weeks in which their spiritual significance is further explored and celebrated. The Christmas season includes, along with Christmas itself, such feasts as Mary the Mother of God, the Epiphany and the Baptism of the Lord. The Easter season continues for fifty days coming to a climax and conclusion with the celebration of the descent of the Spirit on the first community at Pentecost.

The Sundays that are not a part of either the Christmas or the Easter cycles are called Sundays of ordinary time or Sundays throughout the year. Their liturgies build a bridge between the end of the Christmas season and the beginning of Lent and between Pentecost and the first Sunday of Advent. Because the precise number of Sundays in the two periods varies from year to year, liturgies exist for thirty-three of them (although numbered 2 to 34) and are distributed in two uneven groups for the weeks following the Christmas and Easter seasons.

At a very early date in the history of Christianity Sunday, or the Lord's Day, took on for believers a unique significance. It marked the day of the resurrection of Jesus and of the gift of his Spirit. It was a day of rejoicing and celebration, a day for the community to gather, to listen to the scriptures and to give thanks in the eucharist for the saving power of Christ's paschal mystery. In spite of social, cultural, and other changes over the centuries, the church has steadfastly tried to keep alive among its members a sense of the special character of Sunday and of the centrality to it of the community celebration of the eucharist.

Modern scripture scholarship has provided believers with a wonderful tool for deepening their understanding of the Bible. Because of it we now know a great deal more about the religious, social and political background out of which its various books came and about the different literary forms in which they are written. Christians have always seen the Bible as the word of God in human language. Contemporary research has helped us to discern in a more nuanced way than in the past the various human voices that can be heard in it. As helpful as such scholarship is, however, it remains for believers only a means to an end. What finally we want to hear in the scriptures is the word of God illuminating, consoling, inspiring, and challenging us in the here and now, in the concreteness of our own personal and community lives.

The proclamation of the biblical readings within the context of the liturgy is a very special event with its own distinctive meaning. In the presence of God and united by the power of the Spirit with the risen Christ, we gather as communities of faith to praise and worship God and to open ourselves to the divine gifts of truth and life. When the scriptures are read and listened to in this context in faith, God's word sounds anew.

The human language of scripture often strikes us as foreign and not immediately evident in its meaning. It reflects the categories and worldview of a culture far different from our own. Jesus himself speaks like the first century Palestinian Jew that he was. His words, moreover, come to us through the reflections and experiences of different early Christian communities, and finally through the distinctive style and ways of thinking of each evangelist. The task of homilists is to act in some way as translators. They are to build bridges of understanding between the then of the text and the now of our experience. It is their responsibility to facilitate in every way possible our encounter in the present with God's word.

The biblical reflections in the present book are based on modern scholarship without in any sense being technical. Nor are they in any sense exhaustive. What they represent is an attempt to draw out from the assigned readings one or two themes that could be the focus of a prayerful preparation for participation in the liturgical celebration. As such they should be of value to anyone who is willing to put some time and effort into his or her preparation for the Sunday eucharist. They have also been found useful by teachers working with religion classes and members of committees responsible for parish and other liturgies.

As a priest who is called upon to preach on a regular basis, I have found that the disciplined meditation required for writing the present reflections has been a considerable aid in preparing my own homilies. I hope that they will facilitate and encourage others in their own engagement with the biblical texts. What is needed to make any of the present reflections the basis for a homily is a serious effort to bring it into relation with the experience and situation of those to whom the homily is addressed. What matters more than anything in preaching is that a real encounter take place between God's word and the specific group of believers gathered for the celebration. If the present book can contribute in even a small way to helping homilists and others attain that end, it will have been worth the effort spent in writing it.

Much of the following material first appeared in a weekly column in the *Catholic Register*, a national Canadian publication produced in Toronto. I would like to thank the editor of the *Register*, Father Carl Matthews, S.J., for having invited me to undertake the project. In addition to comments on all the Sunday readings, I have included in the present book brief sections on many of the major feasts. Those belonging to the Christmas and Easter cycles can be found in the chapters dealing with those periods. All Saints, the Assumption of Mary and the Immaculate Conception appear in a separate chapter at the end.

Advent

The Coming of God

1ST SUNDAY OF ADVENT
Readings: Is 63:16–17, 19, 64:3–7, 1 Cor 1:3–9, Mk 13:33–37

The Advent season marks the beginning of a new church year. In a way analogous to Lent's relationship to Easter, its four Sundays constitute a period of preparation for Christmas. The very word "advent," which means "coming," reveals the dominant theme of its liturgies.

For many today God seems to be distant from, or at least indifferent to, the dramas and sorrows of individual and collective life. Although they still believe in a creator God, their everyday experience does not speak of any kind of divine presence in their life. While some accept this situation with hardly a thought, others suffer under it.

For biblical faith, God is both creator and Lord of human history. Yahweh is the guide of the people of Israel, the shepherd who has concern for them in their sorrow and adversity. Some of the most poignant passages in the Bible are expressions of longing for God's coming. In today's first reading the prophet begs God to "tear the heavens open and to come."

A God Who Saves

For Israel God is above all the God of exodus and of Sinai. It is he who brought them out of slavery and who formed them into a people. In doing so, he was revealed as a God of salvation. "Our redeemer is your ancient name."

What God had done in the past became a basis of hope for the future. In times of exile and defeat, people poured out their misfortune in prayer before God. They reminded him of his past great deeds and begged him to come to their aid.

Gradually there grew up a sense of a unique and final coming of God in the future, a coming that would bring definitive salvation. It would happen on the "day of the Lord." If the prophets sometimes appealed to this day to warn people and to call them to conversion, they also proclaimed it as a day of salvation and of fulfillment.

The Day of the Lord

Early Christianity was born in the joy and certainty that the day of the Lord was at hand. Jesus had spoken of the nearness of God's kingdom. He had called people to conversion and to new life and had promised them God's forgiveness and love. The experience of the resurrection and of the outpouring of the Spirit seemed to indicate that the end times had begun.

The God who comes had come in a unique and surprising way in the person and life of Jesus. In all that Jesus was and did, God had entered into and embraced our history. The end, however, was not yet. Life went on, and now believers thought of the day of the Lord as the day of Jesus' second or final coming.

The tone of today's gospel is one of warning. Jesus tells us to stay awake; the master of the house is coming at an hour we do not know. While clearly referring to the same event, Paul in the second reading puts the emphasis elsewhere. He prays that his readers will be filled with the gifts of the Spirit and thus be able to live the kind of life that will make the coming of the Lord not a moment of threat but of joy.

The Coming of Jesus

The coming of Jesus is not reserved for the end of time. He comes now and in the most varied and mysterious of ways. He comes in our individual struggles to live religious and moral lives. He comes in the longings of humanity for justice and peace. He comes, too, in our attempts as church to live up to our vocation as the sacrament of salvation. If Jesus continues to come, it is because he is already present among us in the gift of the Spirit.

Advent reveals a fundamental dimension of all human life. We live in longing and in hope; we live turned toward the future. It is a future for which we wait in expectation and which we ourselves are called to build. As believers we know that beyond the immediate future that rushes toward us in the months and years that lie before us there is an ultimate future which is the future of God. God is our future, and our longings and hopes for our more immediate futures are carried by a hidden longing for him.

The great joy of Christian faith that we once again will celebrate at Christmas is that our future has been revealed and in its broad outlines determined, by God's saving act in Jesus Christ. In spite of sin and failure God has redeemed the world. The darkness of the future has been illuminated by the light that shone upon Jesus' human face. "Come, Lord Jesus, come."

Prepare the Way

2ND SUNDAY OF ADVENT
Readings: Is 40:1–5, 9–11, 2 Pet 3:8–14, Mk 1:1–8

The beginning of the public ministry of Jesus coincides with the activity of John the Baptist. Like a prophet of old he emerges from the desert beyond the Jordan and proclaims a message of repentance and conversion. Crowds gather to hear him, and those who are touched by what he has to say allow themselves to be baptized as a sign of their desire for forgiveness and for newness of life.

For the gospel writers John embodies and fulfills a number of prophetic texts, the most famous and moving of which constitutes today's first reading. It marks the beginning of the second part of the book of Isaiah. Written during the period of the Babylonian exile, it is a work of hope and consolation. As in the days of the exodus, it affirms that God has not forgotten the people. He will once again intervene on their behalf and lead them back across the desert to their homeland.

The experience of suffering and evil is always a great trial for people of faith. If God is good and powerful, why are such things allowed to happen? The mystery for Israel was, if anything, even greater. Their God was the Lord of history, the one who in the covenant had promised to remain with them and to shepherd them. Why had they been abandoned?

Console My People

Before the exile, the prophets often upbraided the people for their sinfulness. They warned them of what would result if they did not repent. Once defeat and exile became realities, however, they began to speak a different language. The great temptation now was to despair and to loss of faith. The prophetic voice became one of hope.

"Console my people, console them," today's first reading begins. Speak to their hearts and tell them that in spite of all appearances God has not abandoned them. He is coming, and his coming will be like that of a "shepherd, gathering lambs in his arms and leading to their rest the mother ewes."

Conversion of Heart

From beginning to end the Bible mingles and juxtaposes consolation and warning, grace and challenge. In every case it is God who takes the initiative. God creates and saves, but also lays down conditions and calls for a response. In Christ and through the Spirit, God offers the ultimate gift of communion and friendship with himself. Here as everywhere, true love does not force itself on another; it cries out for acceptance and for love in return. The God who created us without any involvement on our part, as St. Augustine said, will not save us unless we cooperate with him in freedom.

John the Baptist fits into this pattern. By preaching the nearness of God's kingdom and above all by pointing ahead to someone more powerful than himself, his message is genuine good news, the beginning, as Mark says, of the gospel of Jesus Christ. What he proclaims, however, also contains a challenge; he calls his listeners to conversion.

John's is the voice crying in the wilderness, "Prepare a way for the Lord, make straight his paths." Today's psalm suggests what that might entail. It speaks of mercy and faithfulness, of justice and peace. Christ came originally and he comes now not with power and glory but in meekness and in loving service. The only adequate preparation for him is conversion of heart.

Transform the Wilderness

Today's second reading evokes Christ's final coming. It speaks of new heavens and a new earth, a transformed creation where righteousness will dwell. If that is our hope, if that in fact is our future, the text says, we must even now do what we can to prepare for it.

Wherever we look today there is clearly much both within and around us that is at odds with the biblical vision of justice, mercy and peace. In spite of the many good things that our culture continues to represent, one cannot help but think that in some ways we are living on the edge of a moral and spiritual wilderness. This certainly is the impression given by the media and by a great deal of popular entertainment.

Advent is a time of conversion. The great joy it proclaims will only be felt by those who are open to, and prepare themselves for, the gift that is offered the world in Christ. To recognize the reality and preciousness of that gift is to begin the process of preparing a path for it through the wilderness of our times and of our hearts.

Witness to the Light

3RD SUNDAY OF ADVENT
Readings: Is 61:1–2, 10–11, 1 Thess 5:16–24, Jn 1:6–8, 19–28

John the Baptist embodies much of what Advent is all about. For the second Sunday in a row the gospel focuses on him and his role. If last week's emphasis was on his preaching of conversion, today John is presented primarily as a witness to the Christ who is soon to come.

In the early 1500's Matthias Grünewald painted an altar piece of great power and intensity. Its depiction of the crucifixion in particular is both dramatic and expressive. The Christ is a torn and suffering Christ whose passion is echoed in the compassionate agony of Mary his mother, Mary Magdalene, and the beloved disciple. Present also but aloof from the others is John the Baptist. Holding the scriptures in one hand, he points with the index finger of the other to Christ. There is something here that transcends the human drama of suffering and death.

Light of the World

The gospel of John differs from the other gospels in its poetic and contemplative prologue. It pushes back the beginning of the story of Jesus into the depths of eternity. "In the beginning was the Word and the Word was with God and the Word was God." Itself a fullness of life and light, the Word becomes in creation a source of both for all creatures and especially for humankind. In Jesus the Word becomes flesh.

Into the midst of the prologue the evangelist interposed the opening lines of today's gospel. They describe John the Baptist as a man sent by God to bear witness to the light. Not himself the light, he bears witness to it so that all may believe through him.

John's preaching awakened a host of expectations. People began to wonder whether he might be the Messiah. John is adamant in his denial. He points to someone as yet unknown who is and will be manifested as the light of the world.

The Anointed One

The first two verses of today's reading from Isaiah were used by Jesus in his inaugural sermon in Nazareth as reported by Luke. Like the prophet before him, Jesus sees himself as a man with a mission. The Spirit of God has come upon him and anointed him. He comes as the herald and instrument of God's salvation.

From beginning to end the Bible emphasizes the active involvement of God in human life. He is a God of compassion and mercy, a God who cares. Through judges and kings, priests and prophets, God encourages, sustains, and challenges the people of Israel. Mary's Magnificat, part of which constitutes today's psalm, perfectly captures the biblical sense of God. Rich in mercy, he is always ready to save and protect his servants. In his graciousness God uses people like Isaiah, John the Baptist and Mary to advance the divine plan of salvation.

Christ is *the* great servant of the Lord, the anointed one *par excellence.* In him God's saving activity reaches its climax. Christ is God's definitive "yes" to all of creation.

Today's second reading is from the end of Paul's first letter to the Thessalonians. The atmosphere in that community at the time was one of expectation of Christ's early return. In a series of short, direct appeals, Paul begs his readers to live the kind of life that God expects of those who in faith look forward to Christ's final coming.

God Will Not Fail

Applied to our own situation all of today's readings contain both an encouragement and a challenge. They remind us of God's tenderness and mercy, of his saving will in our regard.

The light that shone in Christ reveals the depths of life and light that lie beyond the darkness that seems so often to surround us and our world. Advent is thus a time of consolation and of hope. It is also a time of renewal.

If Jesus is good news for those who are poor and broken-hearted, for those who are abandoned and mistreated, then we as his followers are called to be the same. As the community of those who believe in Christ the church exists in order to embody and to proclaim the life and light that Jesus revealed and was. We do this, of course, by preaching his message but even more by reaching out in genuinely helpful ways to those in need.

Given the continuing power of the forces of darkness and of death, we are sometimes tempted to despair of the triumph of life and light. If the outcome depended only on us, despair would be understandable. It depends, however, on God. "God has called us and he will not fail us."

Handmaid of the Lord

4TH SUNDAY OF ADVENT
Readings: 2 Sam 7:1–5, 8–12, 14, 16, Rom 16:25–27,
Lk 1:26–38

John the Baptist and Mary embody different aspects of the single mystery of Advent. Continuing the prophetic tradition of Israel, John preaches conversion and the need to prepare for the coming of Christ by a renewed religious and moral life. Mary, on the other hand, as the future mother of Jesus, draws us more directly into the inner meaning of the Christmas story.

Both Matthew and Luke begin their gospels with what is known as an infancy narrative. Although differing from one another, the opening chapters in both cases function as a kind of overture to the account that follows. Filled with Old Testament references, they introduce Jesus by showing how he is both rooted in and surpasses the hopes and expectations of Israel. Matthew tells the story from the point of view of Joseph while Luke focuses on Mary.

The word "angel" in both Hebrew and Greek means a messenger. The appearance of such a being at key moments in Israel's history underlined that a new stage had been reached in God's plan of salvation. In Luke's account this is very much the case both with John the Baptist and with Jesus. The appearances of Gabriel to Zechariah and Mary announce that the definitive stage in God's relation to humankind is about to begin.

A New Beginning

To mark the radical newness of what God will do, John's birth breaks out of what might normally be expected. We are told that Elizabeth is barren and that both she and her husband are advanced in age. If the precursor's birth is touched by the extraordinary, this is even more the case with that of Jesus. As at creation itself, the Holy Spirit will overshadow Mary so that while still a virgin she will become the mother of the Messiah.

Mary's virginity has nothing to do with a denigrating of human sexuality or the fruitful love of a believing couple. It proclaims, rather, the uniqueness of Jesus and of his mission. Descended from David according to the flesh, his birth is the direct result of God's saving activity. Jesus comes more radically from God than anyone before or since. This is what is expressed and proclaimed in the virginal conception.

Be It Done unto Me

Luke makes clear that Mary was far more than a passive instrument in God's hands. She is invited to respond and to become freely involved. She does so, knowingly, reflectively. The contrast with Zechariah is eloquent; he doubts, while she, although questioning, commits herself in faith.

I came across a painting a number of years ago done around 1960 by a French artist. It portrayed a serious young woman looking to her right at a hand reaching into the painting and offering her a rose. Although it was entitled "The Engagement," I recognized immediately that it depicted the annunciation.

The painting captured beautifully the theological insight that Mary symbolizes humanity's ability to cooperate with God's saving plan. What constitutes her greatness is that she first conceived Christ in her heart before she conceived him in her womb. Her faith and her active response to God's challenging invitation make her the model of all authentic faith.

Giving Birth to Christ

If Christmas recalls and celebrates the unique moment in time that the birth of Jesus represents, its deepest liturgical meaning is tied up with his coming here and now. The cycle of the liturgical year with its two great feasts of Easter and

Christmas is concerned above all with rendering present the religious and spiritual content of Christ's life and destiny and of facilitating our involvement in it.

In Christ the eternal Word became flesh. In him God embraced a human life and in so doing drew closer to all human life. The mystery of Jesus is inseparable from the mystery of his presence in us. Baptized in Christ, we receive the gift of the Spirit so that together, as Paul puts it, we might become "a dwelling place of God."

Christmas proclaims God's desire to dwell among us and in us. In her faith, courage, and openness, Mary offers a pattern for all Christian life. May the Spirit of God come upon us as it came upon her and may it bring Christ to birth in us. May we, in all that we do, be sacraments, signs and effective instruments, of his saving, healing presence in the midst of human history. If at the end of Advent we are able to make that prayer our own, then we have truly entered into the spirit of its liturgy.

The Christmas Season

A Great Joy

CHRISTMAS - MIDNIGHT MASS
Readings: Is 9:1–3, 5–6, Titus 2:11–14, Lk 2:1–14

Luke's focus in telling the Christmas story is much more on theological meaning than on historical fact. The way he recounts the events underlines their significance. Jesus is no ordinary child. He is the savior of humankind. In spite of the obscurity and relative poverty of his parents, his birth, as the reference to Caesar Augustus makes clear, has implications for the whole of the inhabited world.

That the Christmas message is first proclaimed to the shepherds reflects Luke's conviction that the poor and the dispossessed are those who are most responsive to the gospel. The angel speaks of a great joy to be shared by all the people. The coming of Jesus means good news for everyone.

The word "today" in the phrase, "Today a savior has been born to you," takes on special meaning when heard within the liturgy. Our celebration of the birth of Jesus is more than an historical memory. In and through it and by the power of the Spirit, Christ continues to be born within our hearts and within our world.

Peace on Earth

The angelic hymn, like the liturgy itself, begins by announcing God's glory and singing his praise. The coming of Jesus reveals above all the goodness and kindness of God. It affirms that the God of creation and exodus, the God of Abraham and Moses and the prophets is once again at work in the world, offering now all peoples forgiveness and new life.

The manifestation of God's glory means salvation for us. What God offers is here summed up in the word "peace," *shalom.*

In the biblical sense peace is much more than the absence of war. It has to do with life and joy and fulfillment. It involves the overcoming of poverty and injustice and of everything that undermines a truly human life. The achievement of peace in its fulness will herald the definitive presence of God's kingdom.

The contrast between the reticence with which Luke recounts the actual birth of Jesus and the joyful exuberance of the angelic hosts is striking. Only a word from heaven, a word of faith, is able to discern in the person and destiny of Jesus God's saving action. The word of the Christian liturgy functions in the same way for us. It assures us that in spite of our poverty and brokenness Christ continues to be born in us.

A Light Has Shone

Whatever the historical reference in the first reading from Isaiah, the use made of it in the liturgy justifies our relating it to the Christmas message. It proclaims God's saving activity in and through the birth of a child. He will be a great and virtuous king and will renew his people and bring them peace.

His coming will be like the sudden appearance of a bright light in the midst of gloom and darkness. He will bring joy and happiness and a sense of new beginnings. Applied to today's feast, the text affirms that in Christ the light of God has shone and will continue to shine into our hearts and minds.

The life and destiny of Jesus reveal that God is not distant but near, not indifferent but full of love. We can only celebrate the birth of Jesus because we know how his life will end. Through his death and resurrection, the child in the manger will reconcile us and the world to God.

A People of His Own

The second reading from Titus emphasizes the need for a response on our part to the gift that is ours in Christ. God's grace, it says, has been revealed and it has made salvation possible for all of us. That same grace teaches us how Christ's coming enables and requires us to renew our lives.

The reading suggests that we have to change something in ourselves and in our relationship with others and with God. We are to be more self-restrained, more disciplined, less prone to selfishness and self-centeredness. This entails a more open and loving attitude to others, a greater readiness to do them good. All of this finally is to be rooted in a sense of God and God's graciousness and of our need to offer God praise and worship.

The text reminds us, as the liturgy also does, that we live in the between times. Christ has come and through his life and death has effected our salvation, but we still look to his final coming in the future. In the interim he wants us to live in the world as his people, a people with no ambition except to do good. This was why he came. If we celebrate his birth, it is because we already belong to him and want to renew and deepen our commitment to his way of life.

Family Life

FEAST OF THE HOLY FAMILY
Readings: Sir 3:2–6, 12–14, Col 3:12–21, Lk 2:22–40

In addition to its obvious religious meaning, Christmas in our culture is very much a family occasion. It is a time when people try to be together with their families, both immediate and extended. The liturgy for the feast of the Holy Family in evoking the family of Jesus invites us to reflect in the light of faith on the quality of our own family life.

The nature of the family has changed a great deal over time. In a less mobile, less urban society than our own, children grew up surrounded by aunts, uncles and cousins. Many lived within easy walking distance of grandparents. Today family members tend to be more isolated from one another. Perhaps the most striking development over the last decades has been the increase of single parent families.

In spite of recent changes, families, whatever their size and makeup, remain vitally important and have the potential for enormous good. The more the family breaks down, the more stress is put on both its members and on society as a whole.

A Family of God

The idea of the family is central to our religion. On the broadest level we think of all human beings as sisters and brothers, children of the one creator. To believe that the whole of humanity constitutes a single family provides us with an unshakable foundation for the overcoming of prejudice and racism and a compelling motive to work for justice and peace.

The profound bonds that the first Christians discovered in their faith made them think of themselves as a family united in Christ. They called themselves brothers and sisters and tried to develop attitudes and practices that would reflect their new-found relationship.

Today's second reading contains a series of directives aimed at a small Christian community, which if put into practice would deepen its members' sense of constituting a family. They are encouraged to forbear, forgive, and above all love one another.

The Domestic Church

If ideally the church community is a family in which people experience a genuine sense of love, friendship and mutual support, the Christian family in its turn is called to be what Vatican II described as "the domestic church."

The church at its most profound is a communion, a being-at-one with God in Jesus Christ, but also a communion among people. If the history of human sinfulness is a story of rebellion against God, it is at the same time a story of self-destructiveness. Christ came to heal our alienation both from God and from one another. It is in the family first of all that his reconciling life is meant to bear its fruit.

The family is the primary place for the nurturing of faith. If this was always true to some degree, it is even more the case in our contemporary secular environment. The family is also the place where we are to learn and to put into practice that self-giving love that Christ both revealed and embodied.

The Family Today

Contemporary pressures on the family are considerable. They come from our cultural values and the demands of work, from the changing role of women, from the media, and from the developmental nature of individual and family life. Because much of this is new, there is no easy way to apply the experience and ideals of the biblical world to it. We have to start with today's actual situation, with its challenges and possibilities, and do our best with it. What the Bible can teach us are basic values.

It goes without saying that anyone who believes in God or Christ can have nothing to do with violence or abuse. Every family member is a child of God, a unique and precious person made in God's image and likeness. We have responsibility for one another. Today's first reading reminds us in a special way of our responsibility for elderly parents. It is a responsibility that institutions for all their help finally cannot take from us.

As its members go through various stages from childhood through adolescence to maturity and old age, the family is constantly undergoing change. Each stage brings its own challenges as well as rewards. What is essential is that we take our families seriously and try to bring to bear on them all the courage, trust and love that our faith is able to generate. To paraphrase today's psalm refrain: "Blessed are the families whose members believe in God and who walk in the way of Christ and of his Spirit."

Born of a Woman

JANUARY 1 - MARY, MOTHER OF GOD
Readings: Num 6:22–27, Gal 4:4–7, Lk 2:16–21

Mary's unique place in the history of Christian faith and piety is rooted ultimately in a single fact. She is the mother of Jesus, the one who bore him in her womb, who nourished him, who gave him so much of his human endowment. The more we believe in and reflect on the mystery of the person of Jesus, the more we have to admire and be astonished at Mary's vocation.

Today's gospel tells of the coming of the shepherds to Bethlehem in response to what was revealed to them by the angelic messenger. They find the couple and the child and share with them their experience. Mary takes in what they say and ponders it in her heart. Their words reinforce and add to what she has already learned in the annunciation.

In the gospels Mary is presented not only as a servant and instrument of God and of God's saving activity, but also as someone who consciously and willingly puts herself at God's disposal. She is above all a person of faith and obedience, a woman who questions and tries to understand what it is that God is asking of her.

Children of God

In today's second reading Paul affirms the reality of the incarnation in simple but direct language. In the fulness of time, he says, God sent his Son, born of a woman, born a subject of the law. As a human being, Jesus, like all of us, did not descend from heaven but underwent the experience of human birth. As a human being he belonged to a particular nation and lived at a particular time. Born a Jew, he came under the Mosaic law.

By entering into and sharing our life Jesus opened up for us

27

the possibility of a new life. As a child of the human race, a child of Mary, he became one with us so that we might become one with him. Through the gift of his Spirit we truly are his sisters and brothers.

Mary is widely regarded as a model of Christian discipleship. Human in every way like us, she too received the gift of God's Spirit. In her case it not only made her a child of God but it enabled her to become the mother of God's Son. One with her through that same gift, we are not only her sisters and brothers but also in a certain way, in Christ, her children.

God's Blessing

The first reading seems to have been chosen in recognition of the fact that this feast coincides with the beginning of a new year. In many cultures it has traditionally been a time when parents bless their children and when all of us wish one another all good things for the months ahead.

Although the text suggests that what we have here is an instruction for priestly blessing, it can surely be used by each and every one of us. To bless is to pray to God for one another, to call down on one another God's goodness and graciousness.

Aaron is instructed to pray that God will reveal his face to the children of Israel, that he will be present to them in their lives and that his presence will bring them peace. At a time like this when we naturally pray that God will bless us and our families with health and prosperity, it is good to think about the content of this prayer. We really ought to pray for God's presence and peace even when other good things are absent.

To Treasure God's Word

Cardinal Newman cited the phrase about Mary treasuring these things in her heart at the beginning of his great sermon on the development of doctrine. He saw in Mary a pattern of what historically the church has always tried to do. The truths revealed in Christ are not to be understood all at once. They need to be lived and reflected on and slowly developed.

There is a contemplative aspect to the Christmas cycle and especially to Luke's infancy narrative that we need to rediscover. Christmas in our culture tends to be a rather hectic and rushed time of the year. What we perhaps require more than anything else in order to enter into its spirit is time to think about and ponder what it is that we celebrate.

The phrase, the mother of God, says more about Jesus than about Mary. Jesus is a human being, like us, as the letter to the Hebrews says, in all things but sin. At the same time, our faith affirms, he is so one with God that in him God shared our destiny, our experience. In Jesus, the eternal Word, the divine Son, entered into and transformed from within the meaning of our life. This is the profound truth to which we point when we say that in giving birth to Jesus, Mary became the mother of God.

God's Appearing

EPIPHANY OF THE LORD
Readings: Is 60:1–6, Eph 3:2–3, 5–6, Mt 2:1–12

The word "epiphany" in Greek means a manifestation or appearing. In ancient pagan religions it was an all but technical term for referring to a divine apparition. In the New Testament it is applied on occasion to Christ, both to his final coming and in 2 Timothy 1:10 to his life on earth.

Established in eastern Christianity in the third century as a liturgical celebration of the birth of Jesus, Epiphany later was joined with the western church's marking of the same event on December 25 to form two parts of a single festival. The liturgical twelve days of Christmas represent a unified cycle in which from different perspectives the one great mystery of the incarnation, of the appearing of God in human form, is celebrated and reenacted.

A Light to All Nations

The story of the three kings, or more properly of the three magi or wise men, gives today's feast its particular flavor. In marked contrast with Luke's account, which tells of the adoration of poor and simple shepherds, Matthew's story of the birth of Jesus comes to its climax in the proffering of rich gifts by exotic and distinguished representatives of the distant East, people who are at home both in the world of astronomy and in the courts of kings.

Throughout much of Israel's history there was a tension between the sense people had of being chosen in a special way by God and their conviction that God was the creator, the Lord of all people and of all history. If at times they separated themselves from others in order to maintain the purity of their faith, at other times, as in today's second reading, they were aware that what they had received was something that all nations would one day be invited to share. The glory of Israel would become so radiant as to attract even the pagans to her.

Jew and Gentile

Matthew's account of the birth of Jesus had a special message for the largely Jewish Christian community to which he belonged. By the 80's of the first century it had experienced excommunication at the hands of the Jerusalem authorities. By this time, moreover, Gentiles were flocking to embrace the gospel. In the mystery of God's providence, it was becoming clear that the future of the Christian faith, rooted as it was in Judaism, was to be primarily among the Gentiles.

The contrasting attitudes of the magi and of Herod foreshadow the experience of the early church. The foreigners, the pagans, recognize and worship Jesus, while the powerful Herod, unlike the "anawim," the little ones of Israel, unlike Mary and Elizabeth, the shepherds, Simeon and Anna, can only see in Jesus a threat to his own power and authority.

In the letter to the Ephesians, from which today's second reading comes, Paul proclaims Christ as a great unifying force among peoples of the most varied background. He comes, Paul says, to tear down the walls of hostility that divide us and to reconcile us to God and to one another. The mystery revealed in Christ is a mystery of reconciliation; all peoples are called to form a single body, a holy temple, a dwelling place for God.

A Continuing Epiphany

If the story of the magi emphasizes the manifestation of Christ to the world of the Gentiles, the whole of the Christmas cycle celebrates the person of Jesus as the epiphany or appearance of God in human life. In the face of Jesus the radiance, the glory of God has shone among us. In the midst of our darkness a light has appeared, and in it we can recognize the reality of divine love.

Christmas is a celebration of self-communicating love. God so loved the world that he gave his only Son. Only love can explain the all but unbelievable affirmation of Christian faith that God, the transcendent and holy God, the creator and sustainer of all that is, became so intimately united to a human being that in a child's birth God was born into our life.

A human being like us in all things but sin, Jesus reveals that we are to be daughters and sons of God, people through whom God wants to be present to human life and to the whole of human history. If Jesus is the sacrament, the epiphany of God in human form, then we who make up the community of his disciples are called to be the same. We are called to manifest in our lives the love of God revealed in Jesus. May the light of Christ shine in our hearts and in our faces and in all that we do.

The Word Was God

2ND SUNDAY AFTER CHRISTMAS
Readings: Sir 24:1–2, 8–12, Eph 1:3–6, 15–18, Jn 1:1–18

By way of exception, all of the readings for today's liturgy have a poetic and hymn-like quality to them. Having heard once again the story of the birth of Jesus, we are invited now to reflect on its deepest meaning and to praise and thank God for what has been given to us in Christ.

The prologue to John's gospel is widely recognized as one of the most sublime and theologically rich passages of the entire New Testament. It begins with the mystery of God and with the presence from all eternity within God of what is here called the Word. The phrase "in the beginning" evokes the story of creation. The Word by which God once called all things into existence, although distinct from the Father, is truly divine.

All the gospels emphasize Jesus' role in preaching God's word and in revealing God's wisdom. Where John goes beyond the other evangelists is in his affirmation of the unique relationship between Jesus' mission and his person. He reveals God because he is the Word of God incarnate. More than just a messenger or instrument of God's activity, Jesus is the Son of God in our flesh.

Word and Wisdom

The phrase "the word of God" appears most often in the Old Testament in the prophetic literature. There it is a dynamic and active word that comes upon individuals and impels them to speak and act on God's behalf. God's word makes things happen, furthers God's plan of salvation, reveals God's will for Israel.

As much as the Jewish experience of God's word lies behind John's prologue, it is even more influenced by the biblical understanding of divine wisdom. In a number of passages, of which today's first reading is an example, God's wisdom is personified as a female figure. Formed in the beginning by God, she became an instrument of his creative activity and a means of the divine presence in the created world and especially among humankind.

The reading from Proverbs is part of a much longer hymn in which wisdom celebrates and praises God for what she has been able to do. Our text focuses on her presence in Israel. She was made to dwell in the holy tent and in Jerusalem and to be an inspiration for the people and a focus for their worship.

The Word Became Flesh

The unique claim on which Christianity rests and which distinguishes it from all other philosophies and religions is that the eternal Word of God, the Word in and through which all things were made, the Word that from the beginning has been present to human beings everywhere, has taken on human form and become flesh in the person of Jesus of Nazareth.

For John, Jesus is in a very special way the revelation of God. To see Jesus, he tells us later in his gospel, is to see the Father. The love that Jesus embodies and lives leads finally to the insight that God is love. The use of "Word" suggests a speaking, a self-manifestation. Everything Jesus said and did both revealed himself and the one whose word he was and is.

John describes Jesus as full of grace and truth. The terms evoke the loving-kindness and utter fidelity that Israel had come to recognize in the God of the covenant. In Jesus such qualities are present in their fulness. In accepting him in faith we share in his riches.

Blessed Be God

Today's second reading, from the letter to the Ephesians, begins with a hymn of praise and blessing. Paul thanks God for having chosen us from all eternity in Christ and for having destined us to be God's children and heirs of divine life. The only possible explanation for creation, according to Paul, is that from the beginning God had Christ in mind as the one through whom he would share his life with us.

As the hymn continues, Paul prays that God will bestow on us a spirit of wisdom and revelation that we might come to understand ever more fully the meaning of Christ and his significance for us. Our destiny is not simply this world and death but eternal life and the glory of God.

The very humanity and warmth of the Christmas story exposes it to a rather glib sentimentality. Today's liturgy invites us to move beyond all easy emotions and to reflect on what finally the story is all about. It reveals God's ultimate purpose for human life. Jesus is truly one of us, but he is just as truly God's Word incarnate. As such he renders visible and communicates to us the mystery of God's eternal love.

My Son, My Beloved

BAPTISM OF THE LORD
Readings: Is 42:1–4, 6–7, Acts 10:34–38, Mk 1:7–11

Jesus' baptism at the hands of John marks the beginning of his public life and ministry. In today's gospel John himself is presented almost exclusively in terms of his role as precursor. He announces that someone is to come after him, someone more powerful than he is and who will baptize with the Holy Spirit.

The appearance of Jesus inaugurates a new moment in God's relationship with humankind. The heavens which for so long seemed closed to every cry are now torn apart, split open and the voice of God is heard and the Spirit of God descends. The end time, the moment when God will act definitively on our behalf is at hand.

The heavenly voice proclaims that Jesus is God's Son, God's beloved. In Mark's account, in contrast with the other gospels, the words seem to be addressed not to the bystanders but to Jesus alone. "You are my Son," the voice says, "my favor rests on you." The time has come for Jesus to begin his mission and as he does, God both reaffirms its nature and reveals his own involvement in it.

God's Servant

Today's first reading is from a set of poems to be found in the second part of the book of Isaiah, all of which talk about a mysterious servant of God. Sometimes an individual and sometimes the whole people of Israel, the servant's redemptive mission involves preaching, liberating activity and finally suffering. Our text evokes his vocation.

Like Jesus, the servant is chosen and called by God and is endowed with the gift of God's Spirit. His task is to bring true justice, not just to Israel but to the whole world. This justice will include life and goodness, freedom and healing. In and through him God will establish a covenant with people everywhere.

From the earliest days Christians saw in the ministry and destiny of the servant of God a foreshadowing and paradigm of Jesus' own mission. In a new and unexpected way, Jesus has been sent into the world as God's servant to proclaim and to bring about the presence of God's kingdom. He does this not on his own but as someone called and commissioned by God.

Anointed with the Spirit

As Jesus came up from the water the Spirit came upon him like a dove. Although the precise sense of the symbolism of the dove is not clear, it could well include a reference to the story of creation. There we are told that in the beginning God's Spirit hovered over the waters. It is constantly the case in the Bible that those who are called by God to fulfill some special task are filled with the gift of the Spirit.

In his sermon in Acts, Peter says that at his baptism God anointed Jesus with the Holy Spirit and with power. It is because of this anointing that he can say that God was with Jesus throughout his life inspiring and enabling him to do all the good that he did.

Although we tend to think of the coming of the Spirit in relation to Pentecost and to the activity of the risen Christ, the gospels reveal that the Spirit was very much a part of the whole of Jesus' life. The Spirit was active in his conception but also, as the accounts of the baptism emphasize, in his mission. Jesus and the Spirit are inseparable at every stage.

Baptism with the Spirit

Our liturgical celebration of the baptism of Jesus reminds us of our own baptism. What took place at his baptism suggests something of what is involved in our own. Christian baptism is different from that of John above all because through it we put on Christ, we are plunged as it were into his death, so that with him we might rise to newness of life.

As with both Jesus and the servant of the first reading, we too are chosen and called by God. To exist at all as a human being is to have a personal vocation, a personal destiny. God calls each and every one of us in a new way through baptism. He invites us to fulfill a specific task, to make a distinctive contribution to our shared history.

All three texts emphasize that God takes the initiative, that it is God who calls us into existence and graces us with the Spirit. Not only are we not alone in the world, but our individual and often broken lives have infinite meaning. The words of the heavenly voice apply to us as well as to Jesus. Through the gift of the Spirit we are his sisters and brothers, and, as such, beloved children upon whom God's favor rests.

Ordinary Time: Sundays 2 to 8

Following Jesus

2ND SUNDAY OF ORDINARY TIME
Readings: 1 Sam 3:3–10, 19, 1 Cor 6:13–15, 17–20,
Jn 1:35–42

Today's gospel contains an account of the calling by Jesus of his first disciples. John the Baptist plays a key role. In the hearing of two of his own followers he calls Jesus "the lamb of God." That is enough to provoke them to go after Jesus in order to find out more about him. It is Jesus who then initiates a dialogue with them.

The question he asks might profitably be put to anyone embarking on a serious religious life. "What do you want? What are you looking for?" In our own, somewhat secular age, we might ask ourselves: Why do we go to mass or pray? Why do we read the scriptures or seek religious instruction of other kinds?

People turn to God for various reasons. Some seek forgiveness and healing, others meaning and purpose, others again acceptance and love. John's gospel speaks of eternal life, while Paul refers to our need for salvation and reconciliation. In every case one turns to God not for power, money and worldly success, but for something deeper, something that touches the whole of life and its ultimate fulfillment.

Being with Jesus

Andrew and the other disciples respond to Jesus' question by asking where he lives. They want to be with him in order to learn from him. It is one thing to hear someone else announce Jesus' uniqueness; it is quite another to come to one's own insight and conviction about it.

To be a genuinely religious person in our culture is not easy. The values that tend to be predominant in the media and in popular entertainment are rarely religious or even all that moral. In order to develop a serious spiritual and Christian life we need to create "counter-cultural" spaces in our hearts, in our families, and in communities of faith. It is only in such places that we will be able to hear the gospel and nourish its distinctive values.

The Body of Christ

One place in which we can draw apart and be with Jesus is the Sunday eucharist. In the readings and the homily we hear about his life and teaching and about the way that people like Paul interpreted their implications. In the great eucharistic prayer and by our communion with it, we are one with Jesus in his act of self-giving. Caught up in his saving love, we become ever more truly members of his body.

St. Paul more than anyone understood the depth of our being with Christ, of our belonging to Christ. Receiving through faith and baptism the Spirit of Christ, he taught, we are enabled to live in Christ. For Paul, body and spirit even on the purely natural level are deeply interrelated. That is why belonging in the spirit to Christ has implications for all aspects of life.

In our culture sexuality is regularly trivialized. It is often separated not only from morality but even from any significant personal commitment. Popular magazines and a certain kind of romantic literature suggest that a sexual affair is compatible with marital fidelity. To Paul such an idea would have seemed hopelessly naive. Sexuality is a profound human reality involving our very identity as persons. It must not be isolated from our deepest commitments, whether to a spouse or to God.

The Voice of God

Following Christ means in a special way being attentive to his voice. In this the gospels continue and make even more concrete a fundamental message of the whole Bible. From the beginning human beings were made in the image and likeness of God; they were made, that is, to live in God's presence and to be in relation with God.

The great figures of Israel's history, whether kings or prophets, holy women or judges, are all portrayed as hearing God's voice and responding to it. Today's first reading recounts the story of the young Samuel, who for the first time experiences the call of God. With the help of the priest Eli he learns to discern God's voice. His attitude then becomes a model of all authentic faith: "Speak, Lord, your servant is listening."

To follow Jesus and to be with him is to learn that the secret of his life was his openness and receptivity to God. His major concern, John's gospel tells us, was always to do the will of the one who sent him. May we who as members of Christ's body have received the gift of his Spirit hear and follow the voice of God as it arises out of the challenges and responsibilities of our everyday life. God's voice echoes in the voice of conscience.

God's Kingdom

3RD SUNDAY OF ORDINARY TIME
Readings: Jonah 3:1–5, 10, 1 Cor 7:29–31, Mk 1:14–20

The gospel text for most Sundays during the current liturgical year will be taken from Mark. Thought by many to be the oldest gospel and to have been used by both Matthew and Luke in the writing of their accounts, it is the briefest and in some ways the most dramatically structured of the three.

Today's reading contains a phrase of Jesus that for Mark both inaugurates and to some degree sums up his mission. Coming into Galilee as a preacher and teacher, a herald of good news from and about God, Jesus proclaims the near approach of God's reign or kingdom. What he asks of people is that they undergo a change of mind and heart, and that they believe in his message.

The image of God as king or ruler was widespread in the ancient world. Israel used it to express its faith in God both as creator and as the Lord of history. It formulated its hope for the future in terms of a final and definitive exercise of God's sovereign rule. The ideas about how this would come about differed, but at the heart of biblical hope is the prayer that Jesus made his own: "Thy kingdom come."

A Present Event

What Jesus announces is not an eternal truth but a present event. "The time is fulfilled," he says, the period of longing and waiting, of hope and expectation, is past. Something new is at hand. The God of creation and exodus, the God of Abraham and the prophets, is at work in Jesus and in his preaching.

What precisely the coming of God's reign will entail is not spelled out. The fact that Jesus calls for repentance and faith suggests that it is inseparable from the religious and moral state of the human heart. The gospel as a whole makes clear that in Jesus God is offering forgiveness and reconciliation, salvation and new life. The experience of the Pentecostal Spirit will focus attention on the renewal of individual hearts and on the creation of a new community of faith.

A Future Hope

Jesus' preaching inevitably awakened expectations about what we would call the end of the world. These were intensified for the first Christians by their experience of his resurrection. It seemed to indicate that the risen Jesus would soon return and by his coming inaugurate God's definitive reign.

Something of this hope echoes in today's second reading. The time, Paul says, is growing short, the world as we know it is passing away. This being so he suggests a certain detachment; whether we mourn or rejoice, are married or have many possessions, we should not lose ourselves in what we do or own. Everything is passing.

The sense of the end times and of the transitory character of all things has always, in different forms, been a part of Christian awareness. At times it has expressed itself in strange and bizarre hopes and fears. More positively it reminds us of the future that stands before us and that ultimately is the future of God. It teaches, too, the limitations of all created reality. Nothing in this world including the greatest of human achievements is of definitive and ultimate value. Only in God and in relation to God do things receive their being and value.

Conversion and Faith

What Jesus asks is conversion and faith. Today's first reading evokes a classic tale of conversion, Jonah's preaching to the pagan city of Nineveh. His is a message that as individuals and together as a society we need to hear, and to hear repeatedly. Wherever there are hatred and prejudice, violence and abuse, lies

and infidelity, wherever people trample on the rights and dignity of others or shrink from their responsibilities to family and
society, there the will of God is not being done, there God's kingdom is unable to come. In all such cases the need is for conversion.

In its most profound form conversion both begins and ends
with faith. Genuine faith in the living God, the God who has
turned to us in Jesus and who through him offers forgiveness
and life, is the surest basis for real moral as well as spiritual conversion. It undercuts every form of idolatry; it reveals our true
dignity; it grounds the hope without which the moral struggle
seems impossible.

As different as the world in which Jesus lived and the language in which he addressed it are from our world and our language, his message is as relevant today as when it was first proclaimed in ancient Galilee.

God's Word

4TH SUNDAY OF ORDINARY TIME
Readings: Deut 18:15–20, 1 Cor 7:32–35, Mk 1:21–28

The brief story that constitutes today's gospel both suggests something of Jesus' activity and awakens a sense of the mystery of his person. At the time a synagogue could be found in most of the small towns of Galilee. Its order of service was not unlike our liturgy of the word including as it did prayers, scripture readings and a sermon. This last did not require a priest or rabbi but could be given by any qualified male Israelite.

It was probably within such a liturgical context that Jesus spoke. What Mark insists on is not so much what, but rather how, he taught. Jesus taught with authority, he says, with an inner authority rooted in his person. Rather than simply quoting texts or affirming well-known principles, he had something new to say and he said it directly and convincingly.

A Jew who heard someone speak in this way could not help but think of the ancient prophets. They, too, had spoken with authority. In their words people had come to recognize the word of God.

A Prophet Like Moses

By the time of Jesus the prophetic voice in Israel had been silent for many generations. It lived on, of course, in written texts, in those books of the Bible containing the oracles of Isaiah, Jeremiah and the rest. Teachers and preachers, scribes and theologians in their interpretations of these texts tried to apply them to the contemporary situation. As helpful as this was, however, it lacked the immediacy and conviction, the authority, that had been the hallmark of the prophets.

Many people believed that the messianic times would be

47

ushered in by a prophet of the stature and authority of Moses. This hope was based on an interpretation of the promise of Moses in today's first reading that God would one day raise up a prophet like himself. Although accepting to some degree the title of prophet, Jesus insisted that finally he was more than a prophet. John's gospel suggests the depths of that "more" when it says that in Jesus the Word became flesh. Jesus not only speaks but *is* the Word of God.

The Revealer and the Revealed

The word revelation means literally the lifting of a veil. It suggests that something once hidden has suddenly been made manifest. The word points to the very heart of Christian faith. God by his nature so transcends human life that it is impossible for us really to know him. The mystery of life and of the universe, our sense of moral responsibility, the experience of beauty or love: such things can lead us to the edge of the divine mystery but they cannot help us plumb its depths. For that, God will need to reveal himself.

From beginning to end the Bible is convinced that this is in fact what God has done. Out of infinite silence God's word has sounded. Through Moses and the other prophets it has revealed something both of God and of God's plan for human life.

In Jesus the revealer has become the revealed. His message is most eloquently embodied in his person. The human love that impelled him and that sustained him even unto death reveals the depths of God's love as well as the meaning of human life.

Listen to His Voice

The God who spoke through Moses and other biblical figures, the God who became incarnate in Jesus, is the God of all life and all creation. He is present in our minds and hearts, in the quiet voice of conscience, in the inspirations of the Spirit. Today's psalm encourages us not to harden our hearts but to listen to his voice.

The heart, in biblical language, is the spiritual center of a person, the place where what is most distinctively human is to be found. It is the seat of tenderness and mercy, of humility and love. When it grows brittle and hard, we begin to shrivel up and to close in on ourselves. When, on the contrary, it is what it is meant to be, when it is a heart of flesh, we are open to one another and to the voice of God.

Each of us has his or her own life to live, his or her own story to tell. What we find in Jesus is the key that helps us interpret and understand what we individually undergo. To reflect on his teaching and life and to celebrate his self-giving love in the eucharist are ways by which we deepen our appreciation of what God has revealed in Jesus. They can also help us to discern God's voice in our own life. If today we hear his voice let us respond to it with faith and generosity.

Preaching and Healing

5TH SUNDAY OF ORDINARY TIME
Readings: Job 7:1–4, 6–7, 1 Cor 9:16–19, 22–23, Mk 1:29–39

Today's gospel follows immediately upon that of last week. It completes Mark's presentation of an early and, in some sense, typical day in Jesus' public ministry. The sabbath preaching in the synagogue is followed by the cure of Simon's mother-in-law and then in the evening by a series of cures and exorcisms.

A sermon of Peter recorded in Acts sums up the life of Jesus by saying that he went about preaching the gospel, doing good and healing those who were oppressed by the devil. Its summary corresponds to Mark's account. If Jesus was first of all a teacher and preacher, a herald of God's kingdom, his ministry went well beyond mere words. His cures and exorcisms were signs that God was indeed with him and that God's presence meant forgiveness and well-being.

In the world in which Jesus lived, moral disorders and certain forms of sickness were often interpreted as diabolical possession. Thus Mark's gospel emphasizes the role of Jesus as exorcist. The coming of God's kingdom is radically opposed to evil and therefore, in a special way, to the father of evil.

A Sense of Mission

Accounts of miracles in the gospels are rarely simple. More often than not the impression is given that they are misunderstood and that Jesus therefore must keep a critical distance from them. And so it is on the first day in Capernaum. People are enthusiastic about what he has done and want to keep him there.

Their enthusiasm presents Jesus with a temptation, the temptation to swerve from his mission and to misuse his spiritual power to earn recognition and acceptance. He will have none of it. He tells Simon and the others that he has been sent to preach the gospel elsewhere as well.

In his extremely compressed text it is certainly not by chance that Mark mentions that before confronting the temptation Jesus goes off to pray in a lonely place. By withdrawing and praying to God in solitude, Jesus is able to recommit himself to the mission and ministry that have just begun.

For the Sake of the Gospel

Given the centrality of the gospel and its proclamation in the life of Jesus, it is not surprising that we should encounter the same phenomenon when we turn to the early church. Today's second reading shows how seriously Paul took his responsibility in this regard. In the chapter from which our text is drawn he reacts to various attempts to undermine his apostolic authority. He points to the dedication that he has brought to his task as a sign of its authenticity. He has made no material demands upon his hearers and in fact has been willing to "endure anything rather than put an obstacle in the way of the gospel of Christ."

Paul preaches not simply because he wants to or because he enjoys it, but because he has been called to do so. What enabled him to become the great apostle and saint that he did, was the utter conviction and commitment with which he responded to his call. Making himself all things to all people in order to help them to come to faith, his joy is that he has been able to be an instrument of God's saving work.

Word and Deed

The examples of Jesus and Paul remain normative for us today. The New Testament word for church is *ecclesia;* it means literally an assembling or coming together of people in response to a call, the call here, of course, being that of the gospel. By it the church is brought into being and nurtured. The latter function is crucial. We need to hear the gospel message again and again if we are going to be able to sustain our faith in it and above all be able to live out its implications.

In order to fulfill its mission the church must continue to preach the gospel not only to its own members but also to those beyond its visible limits. Anything less would be a denial of its fundamental nature. This, however, will only be successful if words are accompanied by deeds. The rapid expansion of early Christianity was due to the witness of martyrs and to the magnetic power of Christian love.

In describing the church as a sacrament Vatican II brought back to contemporary awareness an ancient idea. As the church we are, and are called to be, a visible sign, a tangible expression, of the healing love of Christ. It is a sign that both reveals what he has done and invites others to open themselves to it. Our personal and collective failings weaken the church's sign value and by that fact undermine its preaching of the gospel.

Be Cured

6TH SUNDAY OF ORDINARY TIME
Readings: Lev 13:1–2, 45–46, 1 Cor 10:31–11:1, Mk 1:40–45

Mark's account of the cure of the leper is brief, dramatic, and full of emotion. Whatever the precise nature of the skin disease from which the victim is suffering, he is so tormented by it that he throws himself on his knees and begs Jesus to cure him. His plea is an intense act of faith. "If you want to, you can cure me."

Jesus' response is equally emotional. Most manuscripts say that he was moved to act by pity. Some have the word "anger." It is the more difficult and probably the more correct reading. Jesus is angry at the destructiveness of evil. He reacts against Satan and disease and the tragic isolation in which people with serious skin disorders were forced to live. They were seen as both a source of contagion and as religiously unclean.

Jesus' gesture of reaching out and touching the leper went against the human and religious instincts of the time. It shows that the presence of God's reign means the breaking down of barriers and the overcoming of taboos. Jesus wanted the man to be cured but also reintegrated into the community.

Telling the Story

Here as elsewhere in Mark's gospel, Jesus insists that what he has done is to remain a secret. The former leper is to say nothing to anyone except to those whose responsibility it is to testify that he is clean. The man, however, cannot contain himself. He is so delighted with what has happened that he has to tell everyone about it.

Christianity began not with a set of doctrines but with a

story, the story of Jesus and of what he said and did and of how people reacted to him. The apostles initially focused their preaching on the story of Jesus' death, resurrection, and glorification and of the coming of the Holy Spirit.

The story of Jesus is also the story of God. In Jesus and his activity, God's reign is at hand and becomes visible in incidents like the one in today's gospel. It tells of conflict between goodness and evil, between God's kingdom and the powers of darkness. The story of the leper, including his reintegration into the community, is a sign of God's healing and reconciling presence among us.

Preacher and Witness

In telling the story of what happened, the former leper became a witness to Jesus and to the healing power present in him. His testimony provokes wonder and interest and because of it people flock to the countryside in order to see this Jesus for themselves.

In today's second reading Paul offers himself to the faithful in Corinth as a model of the Christian life. Be imitators of me, he says, as I am of Christ. Like the leper, Paul too was cured, cured of his blindness and lack of faith, of his arrogance and persecuting zeal. His desire to tell the story of what had happened to him made him an apostle.

To be healed and renewed in any way by Jesus makes one inevitably in some fashion his herald. The more conscious we are of what we have received from Christ, the more anxious we are to share our story with others. Paul's offering of himself as a model is not arrogance. Through the gift given to him and his effort to respond to it, Paul has become a sacrament of Christ.

The Glory of God

Our text from 1 Corinthians concludes a section of the letter dealing with questions of conscience. How are Christians to live in a world the very structures of which are permeated by paganism? Can they, for example, eat meat bought in the marketplace if they are aware that it was used in pagan sacrifice?

Although Paul rejects all license and insists on the importance of being considerate about the scruples of the weak, his basic concern is to defend Christian freedom. The principle he suggests here for resolving cases of conscience is that whatever we do should be done for the glory of God.

The healings worked by Jesus reveal the presence of God in him. They provoke astonishment and fear and a sense of awe. To respond in faith to Jesus is to recognize God's glory made visible in him. Paul affirms that whether we eat or drink, work or play, transform the world or reach out in tenderness to someone in need, we should do it in such a way as to give praise and glory to God. When our actions are good, they do this of themselves. To do them consciously with this intention is to imitate in a special way the life of Jesus.

Always Yes

7TH SUNDAY OF ORDINARY TIME
Readings: Is 43:18–19, 21–22, 24–25, 2 Cor 1:18-22, Mk 2:1–12

The details in Mark's account of the healing of the paralytic give the story a wonderful immediacy. They also serve to underline the determination of the people involved to bring their sick friend into contact with Jesus. They obviously believe in Jesus as a man of God, a person from whom only goodness and healing can come.

The story culminates in the affirmation by Jesus that "the Son of Man has authority on earth to forgive sins." The scribes, to whom he is reacting, are right in maintaining that forgiveness of sins pertains only to God. What they have failed to recognize, however, is that in Jesus the God of their history, the God of salvation and redemption is present among them in a new and unexpected way.

As important as the healing is that Jesus works, it is clearly in this context secondary to the fact of forgiveness. For many people at the time, sin and sickness were intimately connected. To offer forgiveness was to get at the root of many of humanity's ills. The physical cure is a sign that in Jesus God's eternal forgiveness is present in the midst of our life.

A New Deed

Today's second reading is from that part of Isaiah known as the book of consolation. The people are in exile in distant Babylon and in many cases have given up all hope of ever returning to Israel and to Jerusalem. The prophet tries to comfort and encourage them by recalling what God has done in the past and by promising that he will do even greater things in the future.

For the Bible, God is above all the God of exodus, the God of liberation and salvation, the God who led the Israelites out of Egypt and who established with them a covenant. The prophet proclaims that in spite of all that has happened God has not abandoned them but is on the verge of bringing about a new exodus, a liberation this time from exile.

God, he affirms, is Lord not only of the past but also of the future. Divine love and power, fidelity and creativity are not exhausted. God is capable of doing new and surprising things. His forgiveness knows no bounds. In the return from exile as in the exodus and again in the coming of Jesus, the initiative is with God and God's loving-kindness.

Promise and Fulfillment

The theme that holds so much of the Bible and its history together is that of promise and fulfillment. From Abraham, Moses and the prophets to Jesus and on to the end of time, God remains involved in human history, calling and leading people to their final destiny. The divine interventions are marked by a series of promises that step-by-step are brought to fulfillment.

In writing to the Corinthians, Paul insists on the definitive nature of what has been revealed in Christ. In him there is no ambiguity, no room for doubt about God's relationship to us. With Christ there is no yes and no, but only yes, yes to salvation, forgiveness and new life, yes to all God's promises.

The initiative, as always, is with God. It is God who has redeemed us in Christ and who has given us the pledge of eternal life in the gift of the Spirit. Our response to all of this is first of all to say Amen. The word suggests faith and trust, praise and gratitude. To recognize God's gift is the beginning of authentic worship.

God of Our Life

In their different ways all of today's readings remind us that our God is the living God, the God of life and salvation. The story of the exodus and of the return from exile do not belong simply to the past. They reveal who God is and how God wants to relate to us.

The tragedy of exile taught the Israelites that God's ways are not always our ways. The divine presence among us is no guarantee that we will not have to undergo pain and suffering, or personal and collective failure. What the prophets affirm is that even in and through such things God is with us, leading us to our final destiny.

The goal of history as of our individual lives lies beyond this world with God. And yet, as the life and teaching of Jesus make clear, that goal is operative among us here and now. Jesus is the great yes of God to creation and to humanity and to the ongoing drama of human history. Whatever the power of sin and of our own self-destructiveness, God continues to affirm our goodness and promise our final fulfillment.

New Wine

8TH SUNDAY OF ORDINARY TIME
Readings: Hos 2:14, 15, 19–20, 2 Cor 3:1–6, Mk 2:18–22

There are a number of incidents in the gospels that focus on Jesus' attitudes and practices in regard to eating. Sometimes the issue is the people with whom he shares his meals; at other times, as in today's reading, it relates to the freedom with which he approaches traditional forms. People are scandalized that he is not as severe about fasting as either the Pharisees or John the Baptist.

The answer Jesus gives to his critics underlines the special meaning of his presence among us. Like a wedding celebration it demands rejoicing and feasting, not sadness or fasting. The marriage imagery and especially the mention of the bridegroom came to be seen as an affirmation that with Jesus the messianic times had arrived. The saying about future fasting was understood to refer to the period of the church.

The sense of something radically new is carried over into the two following sayings about patching a cloak and the need to put new wine in new wineskins. The coming of Jesus represents a new moment in the history of God's dealings with humanity, a moment that demands newness of life.

To Take You as Wife

The mention in the gospel of the bridegroom obviously motivated the choice of today's first reading. Hosea's life and above all his unfortunate relationship to his unfaithful wife throw light on the relationship between God and Israel. Like the prophet's wife, Israel too has been unfaithful and prostituted herself with idolatry and injustice.

In our text God announces that he will lead Israel into the desert in order to renew and rejuvenate her. He wants to call her back to her beginnings and to her first fidelity. In spite of their sins, God has not abandoned the people but intends to unite them with himself more intimately than ever before.

The prophet's language could hardly be more moving. In great tenderness and love, God will take Israel for his wife. He will betroth her to himself in righteousness and justice and in utter faithfulness. In the divine embrace, Israel will come to know and love its God in a new and deeper way.

A New Covenant

A favorite biblical way of describing the relationship between God and humanity is in terms of covenant. The word suggests a mutual commitment, a contract, an agreement. In the exodus God called the Israelites out of slavery and made a covenant with them. Although the initiative was with God, the people were called to respond, to keep the commandments, to live lives worthy of God's call.

The language of Hosea is evocative of both the exodus and the covenant. What is new is his understanding of marriage as a form of covenant and as related in a special way to God's covenant. The infidelity of the prophet's wife breaks the covenant of their marriage and at the same time reflects Israel's disregard of its covenant with God.

In today's second reading, Paul introduces the theme of the covenant in relation to Christ. In him God has offered a new covenant to humankind, one not of the letter but of the Spirit. It is written on Paul's heart and on the hearts of all believers.

The Spirit Gives Life

In our text Paul is responding to various criticisms that have been levelled against him and his preaching. People have suggested that he is self-seeking and that he has not come with recommendations from other churches as he should have. For Paul, the very success of his ministry undermines such criticism.

The community itself, alive in Christ, and living out of the fulness of the Spirit, is all the recommendation that he needs.

Elsewhere, in relation to the eucharist, Paul had spoken of the new covenant in Christ. Here he insists that what is at stake in it is not simply new requirements but rather a radical transformation of the very nature of the covenant. It is sealed, not by new laws, but by the gift of the Spirit.

Thomas Aquinas once stated that the essence of Christianity is grace, the grace given to believers through the Spirit. Everything else, he said, including the gospels and the sacraments is secondary. They exist to mediate God's grace, God's life, to us. Without the Spirit nothing avails. With the Spirit we are alive to God and in the very best of ways to one another. It is to the gift of the Spirit, finally, that the new wine of which Jesus spoke points.

Lent

Easter Preparation

1ST SUNDAY IN LENT
Readings: Gen 9:8–15, 1 Pet 3:18–22, Mk 1:12–15

Building on their own Jewish background, Christians from the beginning had a sense of what might be called liturgical time. Once a year, in the spring, on or near the date of Passover, they celebrated in a solemn way the death and resurrection of Jesus. Initially an all-night vigil, it later was extended to include Good Friday and Easter Sunday.

Such a celebration demanded some kind of preparation. At first a day was set aside and then a week and finally forty days in which people were encouraged to fast and pray and to dispose themselves to take part in the paschal liturgy. As the Easter vigil was also a favored time for baptism, Lent took on the character of a period of preparation for that sacrament as well. The close connection between Easter and baptism is underlined for us by our renewal of baptismal promises on that day.

Struggle with Satan

Today's gospel tells the story of how Jesus, before beginning his public ministry, was driven by the Spirit into the wilderness to be tempted there by Satan. Unlike Matthew and Luke, Mark does not inform us of the details of the temptations. His account is both briefer and more dramatic.

Jesus was above all a man of God. His whole life was rooted in and consumed by his relationship to the one he called Abba, Father. Even in his humanity, Jesus was uniquely the Son. He knew himself to be called, chosen, sent on a mission. His life's passion was to proclaim the good news of God's kingdom.

Before beginning to preach, Jesus felt compelled to withdraw into the desert. There he could be alone and fast and pray.

Once there he had to wrestle with the demons, with temptations, with all that stood in opposition to God and to the divine will.

Death and Resurrection

Life as Jesus lived it was a serious matter. He lived consciously and intensely in the presence of the most fundamental of human conflicts, those between good and evil, faith and unbelief, hope and despair, God and Satan. Called by God to live this way, he could count on divine help and protection, but he had at the same time to give his will over entirely to that of the Father. The struggle begun in the wilderness was continued in Gethsemani and consummated on the cross.

In today's opening prayer we ask that through our observance of Lent we might understand Christ's death and resurrection and come to reflect it in our lives. The two parts of the prayer are inseparable. Genuine understanding of spiritual realities only comes by living them.

The first Christians interpreted Jesus' death and resurrection as a new Passover. Just as God brought the Israelites out of slavery and led them across the desert to a land of their own, so in Jesus, and above all in his death and resurrection, God is calling us out of fear of death and enslavement to sin into a new life, a life that will one day be brought to fulfillment in God. There is a sense in which that life has already begun, but there is another and obvious sense in which we are still in the wilderness of temptation and struggle.

Baptism

In the early church baptism was administered mainly to adults. The emphasis, therefore, was on faith and conversion, on the need for personal understanding and commitment. Given the minority position of Christianity and the fact of persecution, baptism was a significant step demanding serious preparation. To provide it the catechumenate was developed, a program of two or more years including prayer, discipline, study, and gradual integration into church life.

Today's second reading relates baptism to Jesus' death and resurrection. It also refers to the ancient story of the flood and sees it as a type or foreshadowing of baptism. If its waters destroyed life, Noah and his family were led through them to salvation. After the flood God made, as it were, a new beginning of creation. He established a covenant with Noah and in doing so committed himself to his creation forever.

In Jesus God has made a new and definitive covenant with humanity. We become part of it by being caught up in Jesus' Passover, by receiving into our own lives its power for life and holiness, by committing ourselves to live its implications. We do this initially in baptism. Our yearly Easter celebration invites us to renew our commitment and to open ourselves again to God's gift. Lent is meant to help us do so.

The Transfiguration

2ND SUNDAY IN LENT
Readings: Gen 22:1–2, 9–13, 15–18, Rom 8:31–34, Mk 9:2–10

The gospel for this Sunday in all three cycles of readings is that of the transfiguration of Jesus. It is as if the liturgy wanted to remind us at the beginning of Lent of the goal of our efforts and prayers. The glory that shone around Jesus on the mountain is a foretaste of the triumph of the resurrection. The path of penance and renewal leads to Easter.

In Mark's account of Jesus' life the transfiguration plays a crucial role. Having just been recognized by the disciples for the first time as the Christ, Jesus reveals to them that his mission will involve suffering and death. They are scandalized and argue that it should not be so. His response is to tell them that his way must become their way as well.

The transfiguration offers them reassurance. In Elijah and Moses the whole of the ancient covenant bears witness to Jesus. Even more significant, however, is the voice from the cloud which declares Jesus to be God's beloved Son. The disciples are told to listen to what Jesus is saying to them.

The Suffering Son

There is nothing more comprehensible than the confusion, even the sense of scandal, that the disciples felt at the prospect of Jesus' rejection and death. After having been with him, having listened to him, having seen what he did, they were just coming to grasp that he was indeed the Messiah, the promised one of Israel. How could the God he called Abba, Father, abandon him to suffering?

That Peter denied Jesus and that the others fled from him

during the passion is a clear sign of their continuing inability to understand and accept the paradox of innocent suffering. It was the experience of the resurrection that enabled them to do so. God, they now recognized, had not abandoned Jesus but had led him through death to life. What had seemed to be utter darkness was, in fact, a manifestation of divine love. God so loved the world that he had given his only Son for its salvation.

The Love of God

Paul, today's second reading reminds us, was overwhelmed by the mystery of God's love revealed in Christ. The fact that God did not spare Jesus is for Paul irrefutable proof of God's love for us. God is truly on our side, on the side of suffering and sinful humanity. All appearances to the contrary, God has not abandoned us but continues to love us and desires our salvation. Here is a motive for trust and confidence: If God has acquitted us, Paul asks, can we then condemn or despair of ourselves?

From the beginning, Christians read the story of Abraham and Isaac contained in today's first reading as a foreshadowing of the destiny of Jesus. Although Abraham had to be willing to offer up his son, God refused his offering and Isaac became the father of innumerable descendants. The story thus became a figure both of Jesus' death and of his resurrection. The deep anguish of Abraham torn between obedient faith and his great love for his only child points to the even deeper paradox of God's handing over of the divine Son. God's love knows no bounds.

The Mystery of Evil

It is never an easy thing to believe in God's love. The reality of pain and suffering, of evil and sin is so overwhelming that at times it seems to give the lie to all talk of divine compassion and mercy. A great deal of the evil in the world is, of course, the result of our own activity. But even this, the more it increases, tends to cloud God's love. The ravages of war that are still so frequently unleashed on so many make us cry out for peace and sanity. In the face of such realities as in the face of personal and of family tragedy, the love of God seems to disappear. The harshness of everyday experience threatens to unmask it as a mere expression of our own longing.

The scandal we feel is not unlike that of the disciples. If we are able to believe, it is finally because the Christian message involves an utter realism about evil and about human suffering. In Jesus God entered into the human condition and plumbed it to its depths. He shared our suffering and even our death and in doing so gave them meaning. Everything we experience can become a way to salvation.

At the end of Lent as at the end of our life stands the great mystery of Easter. This is the message both of the transfiguration and of Jesus' whole life. In the midst of our confusion and of the noise of our culture, let us listen to Jesus as he reminds us of this truth. He is the beloved Son.

God's Foolishness

3RD SUNDAY IN LENT
Readings: Ex 20:1–17, 1 Cor 1:22–25, Jn 2:13–25

The readings for the Sundays of Lent are chosen to a large degree in the hope that they might help us to reflect on the meaning of Christ's death and resurrection and on its implications for our own life. Both of today's New Testament passages do this in rather obvious ways.

All the evangelists tell how Jesus, in an act of holy zeal, drove merchants and money changers out of the forecourt of the great temple in Jerusalem. Unlike the other gospels, John places the event not at the end but at the beginning of the public ministry. It serves as a sign and an expression of what Jesus' life and mission are about.

In the synoptics the emphasis is on the theme of purification. Like a prophet of old, Jesus reacts against what undermines and corrupts authentic religion. He calls for conversion and for a recommitment of the holy place to its true purpose. John adds a new dimension by relating the saying about the destruction and raising up of the temple to Jesus's own destiny.

Jesus Is the Temple

It was only in the temple and under the direction of the priestly tribe of Levi that sacrifice could be offered. If every town had its synagogue, its liturgy was confined to the word. There was only the one temple and to it people streamed from all over the Holy Land and beyond at the time of the great yearly festivals.

A place of sacrifice, the temple also housed the ark of the covenant. In its innermost sanctuary God's glory was thought to dwell in a special way. Many of the psalms reflect a profound temple piety. To go up to the temple was to seek God's face, to enter the heavenly court, to rejoice in God's presence.

More than a prophetic gesture, the cleansing of the temple for John was a veiled reference to Jesus' death and resurrection. His body will be destroyed but God will raise it up and when he does, it will become manifest that Jesus has become God's temple, the place where God's glory dwells.

We Are the Temple

The death and resurrection of Jesus mark a profound turning point in the history of humanity, particularly in its relation to God. Temple, sacrifice, priesthood: these are ways by which over the centuries people tried to relate to God, to seek divine help and forgiveness, to offer worship and praise. With Jesus a new way has been given to do all this. That way is Christ himself.

In the light of the resurrection, Jesus' life and death came to be recognized as the perfect sacrifice and he as the perfect priest. As the Son and the Word incarnate, God's glory dwells in him as in no one else. He is the true temple. If before people went up to the temple in Jerusalem to seek God's face, they can find it now in the human features of Jesus.

What is true of Jesus is true in an analogous way of all those who have believed in him and who have received the gift of the Spirit. To be in Christ is to share in God's life with him. Individually and collectively we are and are called to be temples in whom God dwells. Empowered by Christ's Spirit we are able to live a life of self-forgetfulness and self-giving, a life that constitutes the true sacrifice. To live such a life is to share in Christ's priesthood.

Christ the Power of God

Paul reminds us of the great paradox of our faith. God's plan to renew life and to bring it to its fulfillment is revealed in weakness; divine wisdom seems to the world to be foolishness. Today, as when Paul wrote, there is a widespread blindness to the message of the gospel. Some measure everything in terms of power, success and victory. Others are fascinated by their own capacity to explain the world and to discern the meaning of life.

For those who seek self-serving miracles or who are captivated by what passes for contemporary wisdom, the cross is weakness and foolishness indeed. Yet, Paul says, for those who believe, it is the power and the wisdom of God.

The resurrection of Jesus is God's acceptance of all that Jesus was and did. It is an affirmation of his way of love. He loved us and gave himself for us. Through the resurrection God accepted that love and made it the source of new life. Christ's love has been poured forth into our hearts by the Holy Spirit. What Mother Teresa and countless others embody is more powerful than tanks and guided missiles, wiser than science and technology. It is the fruit of Christ's death and resurrection.

God So Loved Us

4TH SUNDAY IN LENT
Readings: 2 Chron 36:14–16, 19–23, Eph 2:4–10, Jn 3:14–21

Both the second reading and the gospel of today's liturgy celebrate the mystery of God's love. Manifested in Jesus Christ and especially in his death and resurrection, it is a forgiving and saving love. Its intent is to renew and deepen human life and to bring it to fulfillment.

Paul emphasizes its gratuitous character. It was not, he insists, as if we first did something to win God's love. The power of sin and death so undermined our capacity for good that the only way for us to move beyond them was for God to intervene and create in us a new possibility. This happened in Christ. In raising Jesus from the dead, God raised us up with him.

For Paul the death and resurrection of Jesus is *the* great mystery of faith. In the self-giving of Jesus, God's love is made manifest; in the resurrection, that love is shown to be more powerful than death. What took place in Jesus is meant to be reproduced in our lives. By faith we are caught up into Jesus' paschal mystery. We pass from death to life, from alienation to reconciliation, from sin to love.

Believing in Jesus

In his conversation with Nicodemus Jesus makes essentially the same point. He refers to the account in the book of Numbers of an attack on the Israelites by a swarm of poisonous snakes. Moses makes a serpent of bronze and sets it on a pole; those who look upon it are saved. Like that man-made serpent Jesus will be "lifted up," and, when he is, those who look upon him with faith will receive eternal life.

74

The "lifting up" of Jesus refers obviously to the cross but also to the resurrection. It is through his death and resurrection that Jesus will become a source of life for those who believe in him. Once again, the paschal mystery is understood as a sign and manifestation of God's love. "God so loved the world that he gave his only Son." He gave him in the incarnation but also and even more radically in allowing him to die. To believe in Jesus is to believe in God as a God of love and salvation.

Eternal Life

The themes of life, and especially of eternal life, are central and distinctive features of John's gospel. The evangelist tells us that he wrote the gospel that we might believe in Christ and that by believing we might have life in his name. In another passage Jesus says: "I have come that you might have life and have it more abundantly" (10:10).

The life of which Jesus speaks is not natural life as we understand it, and yet it is not unrelated to it. To be alive, to be genuinely vital, is to have a sense of one's capacities and to use them. It is to know and love, to be creative and open; it is to have an enthusiasm for life and the world and to want to be actively engaged with them. Much of this is true of the life of which Jesus spoke. It focuses, however, on something deeper and richer; it focuses on God.

To say that God is life is to say that he is a fulness of vitality and energy and love. God's life transcends anything that we by ourselves are able to imagine or to realize, and yet made in the divine image and likeness we have a hidden longing for it. This is the life that Jesus came to reveal and to share. It is a life that through faith can become a reality even now.

God's Work of Art

Jesus is not simply a lawgiver or revealer of eternal truths. He is God's love in human form. In him God has entered our life in order to share with us something of his own. God has no desire to condemn the world. People condemn themselves by refusing to accept God's gift.

For Paul, God in Christ has given us the opportunity to live a new and richer life. In a wonderful phrase he calls us "God's work of art." From the beginning God called us to live in love and harmony with one another and with him. Sin, selfishness, egoism, violence, hate and all the rest have undermined the divine plan. In Christ, the creator God has turned to creation and offered it the opportunity of a new beginning.

Eternal life is another phrase for what Catholics traditionally have called grace. It is a capacity given by God in Christ in virtue of which we share divine life. By grace God dwells within us. This new life, while transcending our natural life, is meant to heal it so that in this world and in relation with others we might be the kind of people that God intended us to be. We should so live as not to undermine "God's work of art" in us.

Christs Hour

5TH SUNDAY IN LENT
Readings: Jer 31:31–34, Heb 5:7–9, Jn 12:20–33

Today's gospel finds Jesus in Jerusalem on the eve of Passover. "The hour has come," he says, "for the Son of Man to be glorified." His life and mission are at their climax. Paradoxically God's glory is to be manifested in what in human terms has to be seen as utter defeat. Jesus is to be betrayed, denied and put to death. His dying, however, will not be an end, but a new beginning both for him and for the world.

All the gospels refer to the struggle that Jesus had to undergo in order to accept his approaching suffering and death. The synoptics do it dramatically in the account of the agony in the garden. John hints at it in today's reading. Saying that his soul is troubled, Jesus wonders whether he should pray to God to be saved from what is about to happen.

Today's passage from Hebrews points to the same drama. Although he cried out in prayer and silent tears to God "to save him out of death," Jesus submitted and by submitting learned to obey and thus, although God's Son, was brought to perfection.

From Death to Life

The cross is inseparable from the resurrection. The death of Jesus is the moment in which God is glorified only because it issues in a new life. All appearances to the contrary, God does not abandon Jesus but rather saves him. He saves him, however, not from death but through death.

"Unless a grain of wheat falls on the ground and dies, it remains only a single grain; but if it dies it yields a rich harvest." The emphasis here is not simply on life through death but on the fruitfulness, the abundant harvest, that will be the result of Jesus' death. "When I am lifted up from the earth," Jesus says, "I will draw all people to myself." Hebrews affirms the same truth in saying that through suffering Jesus "became for all who obey him the source of eternal salvation."

To Die to Self

If the paradox of life in and through death is true of Jesus, it is meant to be true also for all who believe in him. By definition, disciples follow after their master. In today's gospel Jesus speaks of us as servants. Where he goes, we must go as well.

John's gospel is full of dualistic language. It opposes life and death, light and darkness, heaven and earth. To say that we must hate our life in this world in order to keep it for eternal life is not easy to understand. It certainly cannot mean that we are to hate ourselves and our life, as these have come from God and as they have been renewed and redeemed by the love of Christ and through the gift of the Spirit.

The "world" for John has a double meaning. As God's creation, it remains the object of divine love. "God so loved the world that he sent his only Son." As rebellious, however, as dominated by egoism and sin, it must be struggled with and finally overcome. What we are to hate is not ourselves, but that in us which undermines and distorts what God intended us to be.

A New Heart

What Jesus in John's gospel calls eternal life begins here and now. It is human life in time but as open and receptive to God. It manifests itself in faith and trust and self-giving love. To hate one's life in this world is to die to selfishness and pride, to self-righteousness and self-centeredness. It is to abandon the attempt to find the meaning and purpose of life only within the self and its achievements. To die to self is the necessary precondition for being truly alive, alive to God and to others in an attitude of service and love.

The theme of the new covenant was a favorite one among

the first Christians. They interpreted the eternal life, the salvation, given us in Christ as the fulfillment of Jeremiah's proclamation of a new and definitive covenant. It is a covenant that is written not on tablets of stone but on the human heart. Ezekiel in a parallel passage speaks of God transforming our hearts of stone into hearts of flesh.

In the death and resurrection of Jesus the mystery of God is revealed as a mystery of life and of love. What happened once and for all in Jesus is meant to bear its fruit in us. He is the first born of many sisters and brothers. Through faith we are called to die to self in order to share in his life and destiny. Even now the power of Christ's life is at work in us. May our celebration of Easter this year deepen our faith and renew our efforts to live in Christ and according to his Spirit.

He Emptied Himself

PASSION (PALM) SUNDAY
Readings: Mk 11:1–11, Is 50:4–7, Phil 2:6–11, Mk 14:1–15:47

Today's liturgy is marked by dramatic contrast. Although including a reading of the passion, it opens with a commemoration of Jesus' triumphant entry into Jerusalem. In fulfillment of a prophecy of Zechariah, he comes seated on a colt, a Messiah of peace. People strew cloaks and branches on the road and give vent to their joy with shouts of praise. The liturgy could hardly be more exultant and yet within moments its tone changes.

For every thoughtful person, the cross will always have something scandalous about it. How could such an obviously prophetic and deeply religious figure, one who preached forgiveness and love, peace and justice, be betrayed, abandoned, condemned and put to death? As familiar as the story is, it is important that we open ourselves to what is shocking and indeed incomprehensible about it. Faith in the resurrection and in the incarnation does not explain the mystery but rather deepens it.

Mocked and Condemned

Full of incidents and scenes swiftly succeeding one another, the passion story is populated by a host of figures at the center of which stands Jesus. Presented as very much in control of what is happening, he defends the woman who anointed him with oil, arranges the Passover celebration, institutes the eucharist. He knows that Judas has betrayed him and that Peter will deny him. By the time of Gethsemani he is utterly alone, however, and in the face of what is to come he feels "terror and anguish." The struggle to align his human will with that of God is difficult and is won only in prayer. From then on, the powers of darkness are to have their hour.

Motivated by jealousy and justified by false witnesses, the religious leaders hand Jesus over to Pilate who in turn condemns him to be crucified. As the narrative comes to its climax with Jesus on the cross, there is a crescendo of ridicule and scorn. Passers-by jeer at him, priests and scribes mock him and those who share his fate taunt him. The only positive voice is that of the Roman centurion who seeing how he died exclaims: "In truth, this man was the Son of God."

Abandonment and Hope

Unlike Luke and John, Mark attributes only a single phrase to Jesus on the cross: "My God, my God, why have you forsaken me?" People interpret it differently. Some take it literally as a cry almost of despair and certainly of a profound sense of abandonment. In this view Jesus entered into what was most negative and terrifying in human experience in order by passing through it to redeem it.

Others point out that this phrase begins Psalm 22. Although opening with a cry for help in the face of suffering and death, the psalm ends in an act of trust and a hymn of praise to the God who does not abandon the innocent to final destruction. If Mark wants us to think of Jesus as praying the whole psalm, then he died not with a sense of abandonment but rather with a profound trust in the God who would bring him through death to life.

God Raised Him Up

The cross is an invitation neither to passivity before evil nor to masochism. It is, rather, a symbol of fidelity, courage and self-giving love. It is also a forceful reminder of the power of evil and sin. On one level what happened to Jesus came from without, from political and religious leaders who were disturbed and threatened by what he was and said. At a deeper level, human sin in all its various forms rose up as it were in a final outburst of enmity against the sinless one.

Jesus embraced suffering and death because they came to meet him on the path to which his mission had committed him. It was fidelity to his calling and obedience to God that prevented him from trying to escape. The very intensity of what he underwent became an expression of the depths of his love. The fact that in God's providence Jesus' path led through suffering and death is an enormous consolation for us who in different ways are called to walk the same route.

Today's second reading contains a very ancient Christian hymn. It sees the whole mystery of the gospel in terms of the self-emptying of the Son of God. He emptied himself first of all in entering into the human condition, but he went even further in accepting death on a cross. In response, God raised Jesus up and established him, in his humanity, in the very sphere of God. This is what the New Testament means in proclaiming that Jesus Christ is Lord.

Easter and the Easter Season

God Raised Him Up

EASTER SUNDAY
Readings: Acts 10:34, 37–43, Col 3:1–4 or 1 Cor 5:6–8, Jn 20:1–9

The joy and even exultation of the Easter liturgy cannot help but stir up in us a sense of hope. Death is not the last word, nor will evil in the end triumph over good. By raising Jesus from the dead God affirms the value of all that Jesus had said and done and especially of the self-giving love that brought him to his death.

The first reading is the most explicit of today's readings in its proclamation of the Easter event. It is from a sermon of Peter addressed to Cornelius and his household, the first Gentiles to whom, according to Acts, the gospel was preached. Peter tells the story of the public life and ministry of Jesus beginning with his baptism and culminating in the drama of the death and resurrection.

Peter and the others have been chosen by God to bear witness to what God has done in Christ. By raising Jesus to life, God has established him as the judge of the living and the dead. For those who believe and entrust themselves to the risen Christ, his judgment will bring not condemnation but forgiveness. Peter now understands that salvation is meant for everyone.

The Beloved Disciple

Today's gospel contains the first of several incidents in John's account of the resurrection. Although not including an appearance of the risen Christ, it does end with a reference to the faith of the beloved disciple. The incident underlines a central theme of John, namely that the way to faith and above all to its deepening is love.

The empty tomb by itself is unable to generate faith. On seeing it Mary of Magdala can only conclude that someone has stolen the body. Nor is Peter able to understand even when he sees the linen cloths left behind by the risen Christ. The mere absence of the body offers only an ambiguous message.

In the other gospels one or more angels announces the meaning of the empty tomb. Here the beloved disciple recognizes it on his own. This hero of John's gospel is described regularly as the disciple whom Jesus loved. By implication he also loved Jesus in a special way. It is the intensity of his love that enables him to understand immediately that Jesus lives, that he has triumphed even over death.

Life Renewed

Both of today's possible second readings emphasize the implications for our lives of the celebration of the resurrection of Jesus. If God raised him from the dead it was so that all life might be healed and transformed. To some degree this has already happened, and yet it is something with which we must increasingly cooperate.

The reading from Colossians focuses on the theme of life. Christ is our life through whom we have been brought back to true life. Because, however, we live in a world that still struggles with the reality of evil and sin, this true life remains hidden with Christ in God and will only be manifested at the end. The challenge now is to foster and deepen it within ourselves.

In the alternative text, Paul warns the Corinthians of the danger of corruption arising from the presence among them of sinful persons. What he says of the community applies as well to individuals. What is required of everyone is a rejection of evil and a genuine effort to live in sincerity and truth.

Baptized in Christ

The renewal of baptismal promises, now an integral part of the Easter liturgy, offers a wonderful opportunity for deepening our Christian life. It was by faith and baptism that we first came into contact with Christ's paschal mystery and with the new life it makes possible. The seed that was then sown needs to be nourished and nurtured if it is to bear its fruit.

When Jesus announced the near approach of God's kingdom, he called on people to respond with faith and conversion. The mystery of grace respects our freedom. God's love invites us to respond with a love of our own. Conversion and love, however, are not things of a moment but the work of a lifetime.

The baptismal promises invite us to do two things: to reject whatever separates us from God, and to affirm our desire to love God, to respond positively to his gift of life. Faith is more than an intellectual assent to propositions. It is an act of the whole person by which we give ourselves to the God who created us, who in Jesus Christ redeems us and who through the Spirit continues to be with us guiding us to final fulfillment.

Overcoming the World

2ND SUNDAY OF EASTER
Readings: Acts 4:32–35, 1 Jn 5:1–6, Jn 20:19–31

The first and second readings for the Sundays of the Easter season in the B cycle are mainly chosen from the Acts of the Apostles and from the first letter of John. In telling the story of the growth and development of the early church, Acts underlines the impact that the resurrection of Jesus and the gift of the Spirit had on the apostles and on those who heard their message. The letter of John, on the other hand, is more theological. It proclaims the mystery of the love of God revealed in Christ and calls on us to respond to it with a life of faith and mutual love.

The verses immediately preceding today's second reading affirm that God is love and that anyone who dwells in love dwells in God. Conversely, those who claim to love God while failing in their love for others are liars. The divine commandment is that we love one another as Christ loved us. The letter goes on in our reading to say that keeping God's commandment is not difficult for those who through faith have become children of God.

Faith is our victory over the world. It enables us to overcome the weight of our own and of the world's collective frailty and sinfulness. It opens us to that divine life that makes true love possible.

Believing Without Seeing

Although it is his attitude of doubt that has made Thomas a figure of everyday speech, the gospel account of his encounter with the risen Lord culminates in an act of total and explicit faith. After the first appearance of Jesus, Thomas' position was that of subsequent believers. He was asked to believe on the basis of what the others told him. He refused, however, and became the recipient of a second appearance. By demanding, as it were, such an experience, he reinforced the apostolic witness.

The Easter appearances were not to be prolonged. They marked the beginning of the apostolic mission and of the church. From now on people would be invited to believe in what they had not seen. Faith would be a response to the word of the apostles and the result of the presence of Christ's Spirit.

Sent by Christ

The evangelists tell the story of the Easter experience of the disciples in different ways. They are more interested in unfolding its meaning than in recounting its details. For all the variations, however, certain themes are common. It is the risen Christ who takes the initiative and who manifests himself. His appearances involve a mission; they mark the founding of the church.

In typically Johannine language, Jesus in today's gospel draws a parallel between his own destiny and that of the twelve. "As the Father has sent me, so am I sending you." The word "apostle" comes from a Greek word meaning someone who is sent. Just as Jesus is the apostle of God, the one sent from God, so also the twelve are sent by him to continue his mission. With their experience of the risen Christ the twelve become apostles.

Jesus twice says to the disciples "Peace be with you." Although an ordinary greeting, the repetition suggests that he is bestowing on them the gift of divine peace. It is inseparable from the presence of the Spirit and presupposes the forgiveness of sins. The apostles are called to do for others what Jesus has done for them.

United in Heart and Soul

Christianity has nothing to do with religious individualism. Faith implies love, love both of God and of neighbor. When the apostles preached, they invited people not only to believe but also to become part of a community of faith. This is why from the beginning faith was always followed by baptism. It is the ritual that marks the entry into the community.

Acts tells the story of how people tried to live together in the light of their new faith. Today's reading recounts how at least initially and in Jerusalem they were so one in mind and heart that they were willing to put everything they had in common so that no one would be in need.

Although this particular form of Christian life did not endure, it has remained an ideal and an inspiration until today. Over the centuries monks and religious have tried to live it literally. Untold others have been inspired by it to be concerned about those in need. It exemplifies the concrete love that the Easter faith implies. Such love is the only real guarantee that our faith is the kind of faith that overcomes the world.

The Prince of Life

3RD SUNDAY OF EASTER
Readings: Acts 3:13–15, 17–19, 1 Jn 2:1–5,
Lk 24:35–48

The gospel of Luke recounts two appearances of the risen Christ. The first, briefly alluded to in the opening lines of today's text, was to two disciples on the road to Emmaus. Overwhelmed with a sense of loss, even of despair, at Jesus' death, they spoke of their feelings to a mysterious stranger who had joined them on their journey. Appealing to the scriptures he showed them that what had happened, in spite of its apparent meaninglessness, had been according to the divine plan. The disciples finally recognized him "in the breaking of the bread."

The same human drama of doubt giving way to recognition is central to the account of the second appearance. The first reaction of the disciples to the presence of Jesus is alarm and fright. They think he is a ghost. As it begins to dawn on them that it might indeed be he, their joy becomes so intense that they are now afraid they might be suffering some kind of delusion. Once again Jesus brings insight by showing how his destiny had been foretold by Moses and the prophets.

Forgiveness of Sins

New Testament writers have recourse to many different terms and metaphors in order to express what God has done for us in Christ. Paul speaks of justification and salvation, of reconciliation and peace. John prefers the language of life and especially of eternal life. Luke, both in his gospel and in the Acts of the Apostles, emphasizes forgiveness. Christ has suffered and been raised up, we are told in today's gospel, so that "in his name repentance for the forgiveness of sins would be preached to all the nations."

The first reading, from Acts, shows Peter carrying out Christ's command. He announces to the people the paradox of salvation through suffering and death. The Just One, he says, was handed over so that a murderer might be reprieved. The prince of life was put to death but God raised him up and made him a source of forgiveness. Peter appeals to his hearers to repent and to turn to God for forgiveness.

Need for Forgiveness

Talk of sin and forgiveness does not come easily for many people in our culture. It may be because we are more aware of the way freedom is limited by psychological and social factors. It may be, too, that preachers have been superficial in their diagnosis of the complexity of moral choice. Whatever the reason, the fact remains that the good news of God's offer of forgiveness in Christ does not always touch us as it might.

Difficulty with the language of sin is certainly not the result of any lack of awareness of moral failure. The media thrive on reporting it. The end of the 1980's, for example, was marked by story after story of greed and arrogance. People caught up in the pursuit of wealth and power indulged in every kind of excess, including in some cases the disregard of legal and moral norms. Perhaps even more disheartening were the accounts of family violence and abuse. Catholics were especially saddened by the revelations of betrayal of trust on the part of some priests and religious. The reality and power of sin is manifest.

Christ Our Advocate

The belief that we are made in the image and likeness of God includes a conviction that we are free and responsible. Our freedom, of course, is not absolute. We are the children of our age as well as of our parents. The products of our education and culture, we reflect the standards and attitudes of our social environment. And yet, for all that, we are responsible for our own actions. To deny that is to deny our dignity.

Sometimes our guilt is obvious; we have done something wrong and we know it. Sometimes, however, it is much less clear. We are part of a way of life, for example, that turns its back on the poor or that acts in ways that rob future generations of precious natural resources. Here we may feel a certain guilt but we don't know what to do with it.

Today's second reading affirms that Christ is our advocate with God, someone who takes away our sins and those of the world. The trust such a view encourages should not justify us in our sin, but it should help us in our ongoing struggle to overcome it. None of us is perfect; what we are called to do with our life is to make ourselves and the world less imperfect. No matter how confused our world seems, or how often we personally fail, we must not despair. In Jesus Christ we have an advocate who always pleads our cause.

God's Children

4TH SUNDAY OF EASTER
Readings: Acts 4:8–12, 1 Jn 3:1–2, Jn 10:11–18

In North America since the 1960's there has been a real burgeoning of small religious groups, many of which have been influenced by eastern religions. Through meditation and other forms of discipline, people dissatisfied with their own religious upbringing have sought a more personal and profound experience of what is sometimes called the "God within."

A considerable number of those involved in these movements have been Catholics. For one reason or another their own religion has been unable to quench their deepest spiritual aspirations. It is as if they were unaware of the rich heritage of meditation and even mysticism within the Catholic tradition. The roots of this heritage are evoked in today's readings.

Deeply meditative in style and mystical in content, the gospel and the letters of John ponder in a unique way the depth of the mystery of the inner life of Jesus and of his relationship to the Father, and suggest how through faith we can be caught up in it. The prologue to the gospel proclaims Jesus as the eternal Word in human form. It affirms that those who believe in him become children of God. The fullness of grace and truth that is in him is something in which we are all called to share.

The Good Shepherd

At the heart of a genuinely religious attitude is a profound sense of trust. Neither naive nor unrealistic, it knows the reality of death and the probability of suffering and failure. It believes, however, that even these are unable to rob life of its ultimate meaning. Come what may, life is carried in the hands of God.

One of the best known of the psalms speaks of God as a

shepherd. His guiding presence is with us individually and collectively even in the midst of danger and darkness. In God we can trust. In calling himself the good shepherd, Jesus affirms that he shares in and renders concrete God's shepherding activity. His unique goodness is revealed in his willingness to lay down his life for his sheep. In John's language, Jesus lays down his life in order to take it up again. It is through his death and resurrection that Jesus will become a source of new life for those who believe.

Knowing His Own

The good shepherd, Jesus says, knows his own and is known by them. They recognize his voice and follow him. The relation between shepherd and sheep is so intimate that Jesus can compare it to the mutual knowledge that exists between himself and the Father.

After the last supper, in John's account, Jesus reveals to the disciples something of the nature of his relationship with God. The Father, he says, is in me and I am in the Father. Here is the root of both his action and the mystery of his person. "I and the Father are one." The life that Jesus has come to bestow will introduce us into this divine intimacy.

The knowledge of which Jesus speaks includes love. The best analogy for it is the kind of knowledge implied in friendship and marital love. To respond to Jesus in faith is to open oneself to God's presence. Jesus promises that he and the Father will dwell in those who love him.

To Be Like God

Today's second reading makes all of this even more explicit by using a different image. In Jesus, God has made us here and now his children. At the end, when we and all things will be brought to our fulfillment, we shall be revealed for what we truly are. We shall be like God and see him as he really is.

Bishops and theologians in the early church translated John's convictions into the daring language of "divinization."

The Word became flesh in order that we might become divine. An echo of this can be caught in the priest's prayer at the offertory that "we may come to share in the divinity of Christ, who humbled himself to share in our humanity."

In Christ God has drawn near to all human life. He wants to live within us and to establish with us a relationship of love and knowledge. Only the presence of Christ's Spirit can make such a relationship a reality because it is only by the gift of the Spirit that we are born into the family of God. We then no longer live simply for and by ourselves but in and for Christ and with and for one another. To believe in this involves a genuine commitment to live and to embody the values and attitudes of our elder brother, Jesus, the only begotten of the Father.

The True Vine

5TH SUNDAY OF EASTER
Readings: Acts 9:26–31, 1 Jn 3:18–24, Jn 15:1–8

At the heart of Christianity is the conviction that Jesus lives. As much as we recall and reflect on all that he said and did during his life some two thousand years ago, what is really distinctive of an attitude of faith is the sense that he is alive among us and that he is still an actor in our lives and in the life of the world.

Nothing could be more eloquent about our present relationship to Christ than today's gospel reading. Using a common biblical image, Jesus describes himself as the true vine and us as branches who can only live as long as we are in him. The image has obvious analogies with Paul's notion of believers forming with and in Christ a single body. Jesus is not simply a teacher or model or lawgiver. He is the very presence of God in human form. What he offers is life, a life inseparable from himself. In order to receive and to live that life one must open oneself in faith to him.

Remain in Me

The phrase "remain in me" returns repeatedly in our text as a kind of refrain. It is the condition for life and for fruitfulness. Jesus invites us to dwell in him, to make our home in him, as he makes his home in us. The organic analogy of the vine and branches gives way to a more personal one. Jesus opens to us the possibility of friendship or communion with him. He commits himself to it and invites us to do the same.

To remain in Jesus is to cling to him in faith. Faith here is much more than the acceptance of a set of dogmas or doctrines. It includes trust and love and thus involves the whole person. To believe, in the biblical sense, is to give oneself over to God and to Christ and to live in their presence.

Jesus dwells in us through the Spirit. Just as it was in the Spirit that Jesus himself was conceived and carried out his mission, so also is it in the Spirit that we are born of God and share in the life of Jesus. Paul, who describes the gift that is ours through Christ as "the Spirit that is poured forth into our hearts," sums up his own life of faith in the phrase: "I live now not I but Christ lives in me."

To Bear Fruit

If Jesus is the vine, his Father is the vinedresser. All things, including salvation, begin with the creator God. Through the saving missions of the Son and the Spirit, God's plan of salvation is carried out and human beings are caught up in it. All of this takes place, as today's gospel puts it, to the glory of the Father. God's glory, St. Irenaeus said, is human beings fully alive, alive in Christ and with his Spirit.

A branch that is no longer in the vine is cut off from the source of life and is unable to bear fruit. So, too, with us if we are separated from Christ, if the Spirit no longer dwells in us. On the other hand, to be in Christ is to be able to bear the fruit of a life that is truly pleasing to God.

Today's second reading is a perfect complement to the gospel. It speaks of the mutual indwelling of God in us and of us in God. The sign and the condition of such indwelling is keeping the commandments. These are here reduced to two: that we believe in the name of Christ and that we love one another.

Active Love

To believe in Christ's name is to believe in his person and in his mission. It is to embrace his teaching, to accept his gift of life, to entrust oneself to his guiding Spirit. Faith in Christ is at the same time faith in the God who in Christ has turned to us and invited us to share his life.

The second commandment is that we love one another as Christ taught us to do by both word and example. Our love, the reading goes on to say, must not be mere talk but something real and active.

The love that is meant here is not a romantic feeling or a pious sentiment, but something more profound. It issues in action but is itself more than action. It wells up in our hearts, making us forgetful of ourselves and impelling us to reach out to those in need. It has little to do with the self-conscious and condescending attitudes sometimes associated with the word "charity." It is marked by deference and humility. To the degree that it takes possession of us, it makes us active and energetic in pursuing the real good of others. In a world as complex as our own this involves concern not only for individuals but also for the structures and institutions that impinge on their lives.

God's Love

6TH SUNDAY OF EASTER
Readings: Acts 10:25–26, 34–35, 44–48, 1 Jn 4:7–10,
Jn 15:9–17

Continuing the celebratory tone of the Easter season, the central theme of today's liturgy is once again love. The gospel picks up where last Sunday's text ended. Jesus affirms his great love for us. It is rooted in and reflects the love that the Father has for him.

The mystery of Jesus, especially as it is presented in John's gospel, is a mystery of the most profound intimacy between himself and the one he calls his Father. Sent by the Father into the world, Jesus' constant motivation has been to do the Father's will. In all that he has done he has remained steadfast in the Father's love.

Divine love, Jesus suggests, is like a fire that radiates, like the sun that warms. He begs us to remain in it, to bask in it, to allow ourselves to be warmed and illumined by it. To do so we must do what he did; we must keep his commandments as he kept the commandments of the Father.

Love One Another

His commandment, Jesus says, is that we love one another as he has loved us. In our culture, the word love evokes a host of attitudes and emotions. We use it of parental and family love, of friendship and affection, of romance and sexual desire. Our experience of love varies enormously. In most cases it draws us out of ourselves and makes us focus on someone else. Passing through stages it either grows and deepens or withers and dies.

The love of which Jesus speaks has much in common with our other loves, but it is also distinctive. It is modeled and patterned on Jesus' own attitudes and finds its deepest source in God. Greater love no one has, Jesus affirms, than to lay down one's life for one's friends. At the heart of the love of which Jesus speaks is the act of self-giving.

Paul as much as John makes love the center and the test of authentic Christian life. For him the Christian community is a community of love and mutual concern. Its members are asked to be gentle and kind, patient and forgiving; they are to bear one another's burdens. That at least is the ideal. The model is Jesus "who loved us and gave himself for us."

God Is Love

Today's second reading takes a different tack. It encourages us to love one another because love comes from God. If we fail to love, we remain trapped within ourselves, but if we are able to love, then we come to discern the reality of God in us, for God is love.

The simple phrase, God is love, formulates what in a sense is the final lesson of the whole Bible. If God created at all, it was not out of necessity, but from freedom. God, in himself a fulness of life and relationship, was moved by love to share himself with what was not God. The only reason that anything exists outside of God is that God loved it into existence.

From the beginning human beings were called to live in love with God and with one another. Because sin and egoism and self-destructiveness became so dominant, a new and saving act of God's love was required. This came to its culmination in Jesus. God so loved the world that "He sent His Son to be the sacrifice that takes our sins away."

I Chose You

The love of which Christianity speaks is not first of all our love for one another or for God, but rather God's love for us. The gospel is good news because at its heart is an offer of gracious, freely given love. God loves us, it proclaims, and in the life and destiny of Jesus that love has become manifest and has worked our salvation.

Jesus says that it is not we who have chosen him but he who has chosen us. The initiative remains with Jesus. He calls us to be his friends and offers us a share in divine life. If he asks something of us, as indeed he does, it is only because first of all he has given us what we need in order to achieve it. He asks that we bear fruit, the fruit of a life committed to concrete and active mutual love. By this will people know that we are his disciples, that we have love for one another.

According to the gospel the mystery of life is a mystery of love. We know this because of Jesus Christ. In his human love we have come to recognize that God is love. We have also learned that we are meant for love and that whatever our weakness we can learn to love as long as we remain in God's love and in the love of Jesus. This is the meaning of every eucharist.

Lifted Up

ASCENSION OF THE LORD
Readings: Acts 1:1–11, Eph 1:17–23, Mk 16:15–20

The death, resurrection and ascension of Jesus, as well as the coming of the Spirit, are integral moments in a single saving act. In and through them God reconciles the world to himself and offers us forgiveness and new life. The ascension, taken by itself, marks the end of one stage in God's plan and the beginning of another. The time of Jesus and of his physical presence among us is over. The time of the Spirit is about to begin.

Unlike the other evangelists, Luke did not restrict himself to writing a gospel. He produced, rather, a two-volume work, the first being his account of the life of Jesus and the second, known as Acts, containing the story of the birth and early expansion of the church. He wanted to show both how the church was rooted in what Jesus had done and said, and how its remarkable growth was directed and inspired by the presence in it of the Holy Spirit. The time of the church is the time of the Spirit.

My Witnesses

Today's first reading is taken from the opening chapter of Acts. Luke reminds his readers of what he had dealt with in his gospel, recalling in particular how Jesus had shown himself to the disciples after the resurrection, and how he had spoken of their future baptism in the Spirit. Strikingly, the disciples at the moment still do not understand. They seem to think that Jesus' saving activity involves the restoration of Israel's political independence.

Three times the text refers to the Holy Spirit. For Luke the whole of Jesus' life was bathed in the Spirit. Present and active at his conception, the Spirit came upon Jesus in a new way at his baptism and remained with him throughout the public ministry. Now the Spirit is promised to the disciples. When the Spirit comes they will be empowered to be witnesses to all that God has done through Jesus.

As Jesus withdraws from their sight, the disciples are chided by heavenly messengers. Jesus will return but before he does they have much to do. They are to preach the gospel to the ends of the earth.

God's Right Hand

The resurrection of Jesus was less a return to this life than a breakthrough to a new and definitive life with God. How one is to imagine such a life is not easy to say. Paul speaks of things that eyes have not seen, nor ears heard. Here every tongue stutters, and the most vivid imagery is hopelessly inadequate.

The letter to the Hebrews paints a grandiose picture of a heavenly temple into which Jesus as the great and eternal high priest has entered. There he stands, interceding for us "at the right hand of the throne of majesty." Today's second reading, while echoing something of the same vision, emphasizes more the kingly than the priestly role. The risen Christ has been established at God's right as the ruler of all creation and the head of his body, the church.

Presence and Absence

Easter affirms that in spite of death Jesus lives. He lives with God, he lives for us. Through the Spirit the risen Lord continues to be with us and to enliven us. He is present in the word of preaching and in the church's worship. He is present both in those who are broken and defeated and in those who reach out to help them. Jesus lives and continues to act wherever people respond in faith and love to him and to the mystery of God in their hearts. As much as the ascension marks the end of one mode of Jesus' presence, it is the necessary condition for the beginning of another.

As true and as encouraging as all this is, there is another side to what is implied in the ascension. In spite of all the gifts that are ours through the resurrection and through the descent of the Spirit, final salvation has not yet come. A new time begins, a time of hope and faith but also of trial and failure. Called to a pilgrim existence, the church must undertake what at times will be a dangerous and hazardous journey. It will only end when Jesus who has been taken up will return.

The time of the church is a time of presence and of absence. Even while we celebrate and live out the manifold ways in which Christ is present to us through the Spirit, we are aware how often individually and collectively we betray and deny that presence. We need constantly to pray for "wisdom and perception" to understand what has been given to us and for courage and fidelity to live up to it.

Consecrated in Truth

7TH SUNDAY OF EASTER
Readings: Acts 1:15–17, 20–26, 1 Jn 4:11–16, Jn 17:11–19

With the ascension behind us and with Pentecost just ahead, the liturgy turns to the role of the disciples and of the twelve in continuing in the world the mission of the risen Christ. The gospel is once again from John's account of Jesus' last discourse and is largely made up of a prayer of Jesus on behalf of those whom the Father had entrusted to him.

As Jesus prepares to return to the Father, he prays that God will care for the disciples as he himself had cared for them as long as he was with them. He has entrusted to them God's world and by doing so has separated them from the world at large. They stand now on the side of God over against all that is ungodly, all that is worldly in the negative sense that John gives to that word.

Jesus prays not that God will take them out of the world but rather that he will make them holy, consecrate them, establish them firmly in truth. As long as they cling to and are protected by God's name, the world will not be able to corrupt them. Their witness will remain true and effective.

The Choosing of Matthias

The first reading is from the account in Acts of the choice of a replacement for Judas. Unlike John, who emphasizes the whole body of the disciples, Luke is anxious to underline the special role of the apostles. More than the other evangelists, he stresses the continuity between the twelve chosen by Jesus and the apostles on whose witness the early church was to be built.

As in John the scandal represented by the betrayal of Judas

is said to have been predicted by the scriptures. For Luke the scriptures also indicate that a replacement is to be found for him. It must be someone who was among the original followers of Jesus, someone who can testify to the teaching and activity that constituted his public life, and who also was a witness of the resurrection. The two elements are inseparable.

While recognizing that both Barsabbas and Matthias fulfill the conditions, Peter and the others hesitate to choose. They want this new member of the twelve to be chosen, as they themselves were, by God's will. And so they have recourse to an ancient biblical custom, the casting of lots. This takes the choice out of their hands and leaves it with divine providence.

Love One Another

Much of the first letter of John, from which today's second reading comes, takes up and deepens the themes of Jesus' last discourse. The emphasis in our passage is on love. God's love for us was made manifest in the life and destiny of Jesus. Because, it argues, we ourselves have been loved by God, then we ought to love one another.

As the Son of God, as God's Word in human form, everything that Jesus did and said revealed to us the God who in himself no one can see. In the love of Jesus we have seen the love of God. That love now exists in our hearts and will be brought to perfection in us to the degree that we become loving persons.

By our faith in Jesus and by our love, we are enabled through God's Spirit to abide in God just as God abides in us. What Christianity proclaims is something much more than a way of life or a set of moral and ritual laws. It affirms that in Christ and through the Spirit God has poured his life and his love into our hearts.

God Is Love

Our text finishes with a dramatic crescendo. We not only know and believe that God has loved us, but through faith and experience we have come to recognize that God is love. Here is the ultimate name for God, the deepest truth revealed by the Word incarnate. Love and love alone accounts for both creation and the renewal of it that we call redemption.

Over the centuries people have used many terms in order to suggest something of God's nature. One of the most profound is the language of being. The "I am who I am" of Exodus seemed to justify thinking of God as pure act of being. As dynamic as this notion is, however, it is finally inadequate to God's reality.

God's true name is love. God is an infinite mystery of love, a mystery that initially finds expression in the community of Father, Son and Spirit within the divine life, but which then is manifested in the overflowing love that called all things into existence. The self-giving of God to us in Christ and the Spirit grounds and makes possible our love for one another and invites us into an eternal relationship of love with God.

The Holy Spirit

PENTECOST SUNDAY
**Readings: Acts 2:1–11, 1 Cor 12:3–7, 12–13,
Jn 20:19–23**

Pentecost both brings the Easter season to its conclusion
and recapitulates one of its central themes. The resurrection of
Jesus, it affirms, is inseparable from the gift of the Spirit.
Through the Spirit the risen Christ continues his mission and
ministry among us. Pentecost marks the birth of the church.

In the well-known scene from the Acts of the Apostles, the
coming of the Spirit fills the disciples with conviction and
courage, but also with a capacity to communicate. They are gift-
ed in a way that enables them to overcome the boundaries that
differences in language create among us. What takes place is a
symbol and expression of the reconciling, unity-creating power
of God's saving act in Christ. Ephesians will speak of Christ tear-
ing down dividing walls and bringing people together in such a
way as to make of them "a dwelling place of God in the Spirit."

One Body, One Spirit

Today's second reading evokes the image of the church as
the body of Christ. As different as we as believers are from one
another, we all share in the one Spirit. It is only in the Spirit that
we are able to believe in Jesus as the Lord at all. Through baptism in the Spirit we receive that unique dignity that is ours as
members of Christ.

Even today some people tend to think of the church primarily in institutional terms. For them it is a place or thing to
which they turn in order to have their religious needs met. This
was not the experience of the New Testament. There the church

is consistently presented as a community, a community of people who through faith have come to share a common life in Christ.

The church is the place of the Spirit. Through the gift of the Spirit in baptism we first enter the church and come to share its life. The community of faith is in turn deepened and vitalized through the Spirit's many gifts. These are given not for personal gratification but to serve the common good.

Spirit of Forgiveness

In John's version of the Easter events, Jesus himself bestows the Spirit on the disciples. Here as elsewhere it is a Spirit of truth and of love, but it is also and in a special way a Spirit of forgiveness. Today's reading has often been related to the sacrament of penance or reconciliation. Initially it referred to the preaching of the gospel and to baptism.

Forgiveness and reconciliation were at the heart of Jesus' mission. They remain central to the life of the church. The word of the gospel calls us to faith and conversion. When we respond, God reconciles us to himself and fills us with the gift of his life. In the case of adults this is subsequently sealed and celebrated in baptism. When we sin and find ourselves at odds with God, forgiveness is always available through the sacrament of reconciliation. What today's reading suggests is that the whole life of the church should be marked by the presence of the Spirit of forgiveness.

The Fire of Love

The Holy Spirit has always been associated in a special way with love. In the inner life of the Trinity, the Spirit is, as it were, the bond of love that is shared by and unites the Father and the Son. St. Paul summarizes the newness that is ours in Christ by saying that "God's love has been poured into our hearts by the Holy Spirit who has been given to us." Today's Alleluia verse cites an ancient prayer in which we ask the Spirit to kindle in our hearts the fire of love.

In the liturgy the scripture readings always and inevitably lead into the eucharist. In its central prayer we praise and thank God for his many gifts and especially for what he has done for us in Jesus Christ. As we pray we remember in a special way how Jesus at the last supper revealed and communicated the depth of his love in the words that he said over the bread and the wine. We pray to the Spirit that in our celebration Christ himself will be among us and that we who share in his body and blood will "be filled with his Holy Spirit and become one body, one spirit in Christ."

If in one sense the church exists to celebrate and keep alive the memorial of Christ's death and resurrection, the eucharist in its turn exists in order to foster that faith and love without which the church would cease to exist. Now as in the beginning, it is the Spirit that enlivens the church and that enables it to be the body of Christ.

Trinity Sunday and Corpus Christi

The Life of God

TRINITY SUNDAY
Readings: Deut 4:32–34, 39–40, Rom 8:14–17, Mt 28:16–20

The language of God as Father, Son and Spirit permeates our religious life. It was in God's threefold name that we were baptized, that our creeds are structured, that we bless ourselves. The eucharist, the central act of our faith, is in the form of a hymn of praise and thanksgiving addressed to the Father, through the Son, in the power of the Holy Spirit.

Christianity inherited from the Jewish tradition a profound sense of the radical oneness of God. The vitality and variety that so mark our world, far from reflecting a multiplicity of gods as many spontaneously thought, give witness to the inexhaustible power and goodness of a transcendent creator. The Lord is God and there is no other.

What is most distinctive of the religious experience of the people of the Bible, however, is not simply that God is creator but that he became involved in their history. Today's first reading evokes the heart of Israel's faith. It marvels that the voice of God has sounded among them and made of them God's own people. The creator God is the Lord of human history.

Word and Son

It was against this background of Israel's paradoxical faith in God both as distant and near, as transcendent creator and saving presence, that Jesus preached and that people came to believe in him. He spoke of God as at hand, as offering forgiveness and renewal of life. What he said and did was rooted in a singularly intimate experience of God. He called God "Abba," a phrase suggesting the trusting, loving attitude of a child to its father.

It was only in the light of the death and resurrection of Jesus and in the power of the new spiritual experience unleashed by that event that Christian faith was really born. It focused initially on what God had done for humankind in Christ, but it also, and from the beginning, included a sense of Jesus' own uniqueness.

The history of God's presence to Israel had reached a new and unexpected intensity in the human life and destiny of Jesus. He is the beloved of God, God's only Son, the eternal Word of God in human form.

The Spirit of Jesus

Today's second reading is absolutely typical in its conviction about the centrality of the Spirit to any authentic Christian faith. Through the gift of the Spirit, we are caught up in the life of Jesus and are able with him to cry "Abba," Father.

When we refer to the myths people live by, what we mean is not something unreal, but profoundly real. It points to those things that touch us most deeply, that motivate and mold our lives. Some people live by the myth of power or pleasure or wealth. To be a Christian is to be animated by the "myth" of Christ. It is to be so filled with the reality of Jesus that his life and values, his very person live in us and influence all that we do.

The Spirit of Jesus, working mysteriously in our hearts, makes of us children of God and sisters and brothers of Christ and of one another.

The Living God

In spite of the apparently growing secularity of our culture, one encounters individuals, in the arts community and elsewhere, who rebel against a one-dimensional world. They affirm that there is something that transcends everyday life, that bursts the confines of science and technology. Theirs is a dawning awareness of the world of mystery.

Such intimations of God need to be nurtured and given more precise content. For a Christian the mystery that surrounds and permeates life is the mystery of the living God. As easily as we might use the word God, we know that its content always escapes us. As little as we know of God, however, we do as Christians know something that is both consoling and illuminating. We know that the one God is Father, Son and Spirit.

To think of God is to think of the ground and goal of all that is, it is to think of God as creator and sustainer, as the holy mystery that permeates and gives meaning to our life. To think of God is also to think of Jesus Christ. In his life and teaching and above all in his person, God revealed the depths of his love. To think of God, finally, is to think of the Spirit, the life-giving power of God who makes both the Father and the Son as present to us as we are to ourselves.

One Body in Christ

SOLEMNITY OF THE BODY AND BLOOD OF CHRIST
Readings: Ex 24:3–8, Heb 9:11–15, Mk 14:12–16, 22–26

The eucharist stands at the heart of Christian life. A memorial that both recalls and renders present the life-giving power of Jesus' death and resurrection, it was originally celebrated within the context of a community meal. By the end of the first century it was separated from the meal and joined to something very like our present liturgy of the word. At the same time it took on the form of an extended hymn of praise and thanksgiving. This gave it the name most commonly used today, eucharist, a Greek word meaning thanksgiving.

As powerfully as the eucharist touches us as individuals, it has always had a special relationship to the broader community of faith. The traditional name for today's feast, Corpus Christi, the body of Christ, evokes three inseparable realities: the historical person of Jesus, his sacramental presence, and the church. As the body of Christ, the church is called into being by the life and teaching of Jesus. It is animated and sustained by his continuing presence to it in the Spirit. Its life is constantly renewed by its celebration of the eucharist.

God's Covenant with Israel

A common thread running through today's readings is the theme of covenant. Jesus identifies the wine as his blood, "the blood of the covenant, which is to be poured out for many." For people steeped in the traditions of Israel, the reference was as obvious as it was revolutionary. The word covenant pointed to the Bible's most cherished way of thinking about God's relationship to his people.

Covenant suggests a pact or agreement, a promise, a commitment. It was used to describe the promise that God made with Abraham and, more importantly, the relationship that he established with Israel through Moses.

The story of the exodus is inseparable from what took place on Sinai. If God freed the people from slavery, it was to bind them to himself. Moses sealed the covenant, as the first reading tells us, by offering sacrifice and by sprinkling on the altar and on the assembled people "the blood of the covenant."

A New Covenant

The letter to the Hebrews, from which our second reading is taken, is unique in the centrality it gives to the themes of sacrifice and priesthood. Although Jesus was not a priest in the Jewish sense of the word, Christians soon came to see how in a surpassing way he fulfilled all that ritual and cult, priesthood and temple had ever been meant to achieve.

His priesthood was not played out in the temple in Jerusalem or in any other earthly temple. By his life of fidelity and self-giving love, and especially by his continuing commitment even in the face of death, he offered the perfect sacrifice of himself. Brought into the heavenly temple through the resurrection, he remains there forever as a priest interceding on our behalf.

Hebrews calls Jesus the mediator of a new covenant. By his blood, that is, by his self-giving love, he became the instrument by which God renewed and deepened the relationship that he wants to have with humankind. In Jesus God has committed himself to us and calls upon us to commit ourselves to him.

Renewing the Covenant

The great sin for the Israelites was to forget, to forget what God had done for them and to forget their commitments to him. The prophets, acting as the conscience of the nation, recalled the covenant and forced people to see how their behavior undermined it. At special moments in Israel's history, the covenant itself was renewed.

There is a sense in which in every eucharist we renew the covenant that God has made with us in Christ. We remember Jesus' life and death and how he both interpreted and delivered them into our hands at the last supper. By sharing in the eucharist we open ourselves to his gift and recommit ourselves to live it in our daily life.

God's covenant is with all of humankind but in a special way with those who respond to it in faith. The eucharist challenges our sense of church. We who are many eat of the one bread and become ourselves one body in Christ. A community that regularly celebrates the eucharist and yet fails to grow in mutual knowledge, love and service, is failing in its vocation. Like Israel of old, such a community needs to hear the challenge of the prophetic voice calling it to conversion and to a life worthy of the covenant that it, in fact, renews and celebrates.

Ordinary Time: Sundays 9 to 34

Master of the Sabbath

9TH SUNDAY IN ORDINARY TIME
Readings: Deut 5:12–15, 2 Cor 4:6–11, Mk 2:23–3:6

Today's gospel contains two stories, both of which present Jesus in a situation of conflict with the religious establishment of his time. Over the centuries an increased emphasis had been given to the precise and detailed observance of the sabbath rest. Conformity with the law in this regard offered a clear and public indication of commitment to the religion of the covenant.

In the first story, people complain that Jesus' disciples are disregarding the prohibition of work on the sabbath by plucking heads of grain. In a typically rabbinical way Jesus argues from a different but analogous breach of the law by David. Going further, he enunciates a principle about the sabbath being made for humankind and not vice versa that relativizes the law and undercuts all legalistic approaches to it.

The following phrase carries the argument to a new level. What ultimately is at stake in the conflict is not two different legal interpretations, but the presence of someone with authority over the law itself. As the mysterious Son of man associated in Israel's hopes with the definitive coming of God's reign, Jesus stands above the law of Moses. He is master of the sabbath.

God's Glory in Christ

The implicit christology of Mark's story is made explicit by Paul in the first reading. It comes from a longer text in which the apostle defends his ministry against various charges. Some of these relate to Moses and to the glory that surrounded him when he brought God's law to the people. Paul's paltry humanity and public failures are hardly indicative that he has been entrusted with a comparable ministry.

In response Paul contrasts Moses not with himself but with Christ. It is in the face of Christ that God's glory is now manifest. He has inaugurated a new covenant and brought a revelation that renders the law given to Moses obsolete.

The God of creation, the God who originally brought light out of darkness, has poured the light of faith into our hearts so that we are able to recognize the glory revealed in Christ. What Paul teaches by means of the imagery of light and glory, Mark affirms in the form of stories. In Jesus God is revealing and doing something new. The challenge to us is to recognize it.

To Do Good

The second of Mark's stories is dramatically told. Jesus is in a synagogue on the sabbath, and there is a man present with a withered hand. Some of those watching and wondering what will happen are anything but sympathetic. Here is a case where one cannot appeal to any necessity.

Knowing their thoughts, Jesus becomes angry. He is angry because they are obstinate, because they are blind, because they have hearts of stone. What they don't see is human need and the possibility that God's extravagant graciousness might in and through Jesus respond to it. All they can see is the law and the possibility of catching Jesus out in regard to it.

According to the rabbis, it was permitted to save someone from death on the sabbath. What Jesus does in this case is to go further. By curing the man he does not save his life, but he makes it better, easier, more fulfilling. The gospel miracles are signs of the breaking in of God's reign. Here that reign is revealed in terms of healing and of merciful generosity.

Earthen Vessels

Christianity was born in the conviction that the God of creation and of exodus was in a new way active in the midst of humanity, bringing it a step nearer to salvation and redemption. In Jesus, God's glory was revealed as a power for life and healing. His coming meant the establishment of a new covenant, the beginning of a new creation, the fulfillment of human hopes.

If this was the faith of the early church, the form of its life seemed to belie it. It was a small community of ordinary people who were divided among themselves and scorned and rejected by those around them. No one more eloquently articulated the pathos and the paradox of this situation than Paul.

We are earthen vessels, jars of clay, Paul says, so that it will be clear to us and to everyone that the power for life and renewal present among us is not from us but from God. Paul glories in his suffering because it enables him to share in the death of Jesus. That death, however, is inseparable from Christ's risen life. The faith and love, the fidelity and trust of believers in the face of trials and persecutions bear witness to the presence in them of the life of Jesus.

The True Family of Jesus

10TH SUNDAY OF ORDINARY TIME
Readings: Gen 3:9–15, 2 Cor 4:13–5:1, Mk 3:20–35

In his version of the gospel story, Mark puts a greater emphasis on what Jesus did than on what he said. The meaning, for example, of his preaching about the nearness of God's kingdom is suggested above all by his miracles and acts of healing, many of which are presented as exorcisms. For Mark, Jesus is a divine figure, filled with the Spirit of God, doing battle on God's behalf against Satan and the spirits of darkness.

This sense of conflict comes to the fore in today's reading. People are stirred up and follow Jesus around to the point that he is unable even to eat. His relatives find what is happening bizarre; they think that he is mad and try to stop him. The religious and scholarly leaders of the community go even further. They announce that he is possessed by the devil.

For Jesus, the charge that he works his cures and exorcisms by the power of Satan is both nonsense and blasphemy. It is nonsense because all that Jesus is and stands for is clearly on the side of God and of human well-being. It is blasphemous because it implies a rejection of the Spirit that is at work in him. The brief parable that Jesus tells affirms that his actions are eloquent enough to make clear on whose side he stands.

The Family of Jesus

The arrival of Jesus' mother and "brothers," a term understood in the Catholic tradition to refer to cousins, provokes a telling remark from Jesus. Blood relationships as such are not, for him, what is finally significant. Those who do God's will are his sisters and brothers and mother. If Jesus is the great enemy of what is evil, he is the friend of those who pursue what is good.

His disciples are invited to share with him the experience of a new family, the family of God.

Today's second reading provides a moving glimpse into what finally matters for Paul. He loves and is committed to both the risen Christ and those to whom he has preached. No matter what he has to suffer it is as nothing as long as he can continue to be of service both to the gospel and to the community of faith.

Paul's sense of commitment grows stronger even as his health and energy decline. The hope that sustains him is beautifully expressed: "We know that when the tent that we live in on earth is folded up, there is a house built by God for us, an everlasting home." The family of Jesus will have no end.

The Power of Evil

Today's first reading describes the poignant moment after the sin of Adam and Eve when God confronts them and they are forced to recognize and admit what they have done. In a typical response, the man blames the woman while she blames the tempter.

The Bible has a deep sense of the power of evil at work in the world. If Genesis sees it embodied in the serpent, other texts will portray it as a monster hidden in the depths of the sea or as a great dragon against which God's angels will fight. Whatever the image, the reality is, Paul will say, that the struggle between good and evil, creation and chaos, involves not only individual persons but the whole of the spiritual world.

If the Bible stresses the reality of evil, it stresses even more the saving will of God. The Genesis text points in a mysterious way to the final triumph of humanity over the tempter. It predicts an ongoing enmity between the woman and her offspring and the serpent; in the end the serpent's head will be crushed. Christians came to read the text as referring to Jesus.

Doing God's Will

Made in God's image and likeness, human beings from the beginning were called to live in peace and communion with one another and with God. The story of Adam and Eve, however simple it might sound in itself, affirms a profound human truth. The gift of freedom entails the possibility of sin.

Desiring, in the words of Genesis, to be like God, desiring to free themselves from God's will and to make their own desires and longings the norm for their moral behavior, they turned their backs on God and embraced a way of life the fruits of which are all around us.

Rejecting friendship with God people experienced a fundamental alienation not only from God but also from themselves and from one another. Jesus came to call us back to our true destiny. As a new Adam he invites us to identify with him, to become his sisters and brothers. What he asks of us is what God has always asked of humankind, that we seek to discern and try to follow to the best of our ability the will of God.

Teaching by Parables

11TH SUNDAY OF ORDINARY TIME
Readings: Ez 17:22–24, 2 Cor 5:6–10, Mk 4:26–34

One of the most distinctive features of the teaching of Jesus is his use of parables. Whether a single metaphor or a more developed story, they provoke interest and once heard tend to stick in our memory. On one level we grasp them immediately and intuitively; on another level, however, their effect is more subtle. There is something mysterious about them, something that draws us back to them in the hope of deeper understanding.

The material Jesus used for his parables could not have been simpler or more commonplace. He spoke of fathers and mothers, of fields and treasures, of planting and fishing. At this level everyone then and most people today could and can follow what he said. What gives them their aura of mystery is that what they are finally all about is God and the hidden meaning of human life as it is lived out in God's presence.

Central to Jesus' preaching was the idea of the kingdom or reign of God. He proclaimed it as near, as in some sense already present. Through what Jesus said and did people were being invited to become aware of it and to respond to it.

Seed Grows

Most of the relatively few parables in the gospel of Mark are contained in a single chapter and have to do with the sowing and growing of seed and with the natural wonder of an abundant harvest. What Jesus meant on first telling them has to be understood in terms of his life and of the reaction of people to his ministry. When they were told again after his death and resurrection, their meaning shifted as it had to if they were to speak to their new hearers. They mean something different again today to us as we think about them in the context of our culture and of our individual lives.

The kingdom of God, grace, God's presence, is like seed that sprouts and grows and bears its fruit whether we sleep or work, worry or rejoice, think about it or not. In spite of our scientific culture, there is still something wonderfully mysterious and hidden about the inner vitality of living things.

The first parable is about trust and confidence. No matter how things might look, no matter how we might feel, the seed of grace is alive in the world and in people and it is growing.

Small Beginnings

The parable of the mustard seed underlines the contrast between the smallness of beginnings and the abundance of the final outcome. Jesus appeared in what from the economic and cultural centers of the day would have been thought of as little more than a backwater. What he said in Galilee had certainly no immediate impact in Rome or Alexandria. Even in his own country he had relatively little success. And yet, as a mustard seed....

Every day the international media bombard us with stories of war and famine, of assassination and repression. Closer to home we are made aware of the growing phenomenon of violence and abuse in our homes and on our streets. It is easy to become fixated and even depressed by these larger patterns of what can and does go wrong and forget what is within our own reach.

The things that we can do seem small and relatively insignificant. They are like mustard seeds, so tiny in themselves as to be derisive, and yet so full of promise that if we were to act on them we would in fact make a difference.

Trust and Confidence

Genuine faith is inseparable from an attitude of hope. To believe in God is at the same time to believe in the radical goodness and meaningfulness of creation. Faith in Jesus Christ, on the other hand, necessarily entails faith in the power for good that he unleashed. The kingdom, the presence of God, is among us and is having its effect in quiet and mysterious ways. Here are grounds for the kind of confidence that Paul proclaims in today's second reading. Whether he lives or whether he dies, he says, it makes no difference. Faith has filled him with confidence.

Christian hope should never be selfish or self-centered. God's grace is offered not only to us but to all people, and in mysterious and sometimes invisible ways it is at work in them. Today's parables invite us to be people of hope. Our hope, however, must expand beyond ourselves to embrace the whole world. We must hope in a special way for our children, for all those who for various reasons have apparently turned away from or who have not yet really heard the gospel message. They, too, are being worked by God's grace.

A New Creation

12TH SUNDAY IN ORDINARY TIME
Readings: Job 38:1, 8–11, 2 Cor 5:14–17, Mk 4:35–41

On each of the last three Sundays the second reading has been taken from a section of 2 Corinthians in which St. Paul offers an apologia for himself and his ministry. In a remarkably personal and deeply felt response to various critics, he both insists on the unique grace that is his as an apostle of Christ and admits his own profound sense of weakness and vulnerability. "We hold this treasure in earthen vessels to show that the transcendent power belongs to God and not to us."

Today's second reading marks the prelude to a famous passage in which Paul sums up God's saving act in Christ and his own ministry in terms of reconciliation. Our text reveals how for Paul the meaning of everything, including his own life, was from the moment of his conversion centered on Christ. It is the love of Christ, the love that Christ embodied and manifested, that overwhelms, controls, impels Paul in all that he does.

Death and Resurrection

There are many ways of approaching the mystery and the meaning of the life and ministry of Jesus. Some focus on his preaching of the inbreaking of the kingdom of God and on the way that his reaching out to the poor and the marginalized manifest its implications. Others are captivated by the great fact of the incarnation: in Jesus the Word of God took on human form and in doing so renewed all of humanity from within.

Paul did not know the historical Jesus and rarely refers to the details of his life. What constitutes the center of his faith is Jesus' death and resurrection. Together they form a single saving event, an event that is rooted in and proclaims the triumph of love.

Love motivated Jesus in all that he did, including his fidelity in the face of death. God's love for Jesus and for all of humanity responded to Jesus' death by the gift of the resurrection. Faith in this twofold love grounds Paul's identity both as Christian and as apostle. Nothing, he says, either in this world or the next, "will ever separate us from the love of God in Christ Jesus our Lord."

Love of Christ

In defending his apostolic ministry, Paul makes clear that all his actions have been motivated by the love of Christ. Faith implies a call to the imitation of the life and attitudes of Jesus. This imitation is neither mechanical nor purely external. Through faith the Spirit of the risen Christ has been poured into our hearts enabling Christ, in some sense, to live in us.

Elsewhere Paul puts it this way: "I have been crucified with Christ; it is no longer I who live but Christ who lives in me." Something new has come about; it has modified the way Paul judges and acts. "I live now by faith in the Son of God who loved me and gave himself for me" (Gal 2,20).

Paul loves to play with the themes of death and life. If Christ died, then in some way all have died with him. They have died to sin and death. If Christ lives, it is so that all will live a new life in him, a life of freedom and love, a life responsive to the Spirit.

The New Is Here

For Paul something really happened in Christ, something that affects all of humanity and in a special way those who respond to the gospel message in faith. He refers to it as justification and reconciliation, as redemption and salvation. In today's text he calls it a new creation.

The God who raised Jesus from the dead is the creator God. His power and concern extend to all that is. In Christ God reaffirms his commitment to the world and begins the process of restoring it to what it was intended to be from the beginning. The prophets had looked forward to a day when God would make all things new. In the eyes of Christian faith that day, although not fully here, has already begun.

For those who are in Christ, a narrowly secular life or merely secular way of judging is no longer adequate. By faith we know that there is more to life than natural reason and science can imagine. That "more" has to do with the reality of God and with our capacity to be in a relationship of friendship and love with him. This is what has become possible in Christ and through the gift of his Spirit. Christ is the new Adam, the beginning of a new humanity. It is crucial both for our own salvation and for the good of the world that the newness that is ours in Christ be reflected in our lives.

Christ the Healer

13TH SUNDAY IN ORDINARY TIME
Readings: Wis 1:13–15, 2:23–24, 2 Cor 8:7, 9, 13-15,
Mk 5:21–43

The two miracle stories in today's gospel celebrate the healing and life-giving power of God present in Jesus. Like parables
in action they suggest some of the implications of his preaching
about the kingdom of God. It means salvation and wholeness,
especially for the weak and the powerless. The fact that the miracles benefit a woman and a twelve-year-old girl underlines how
Jesus transcended the gender barriers of his day.

The story of the woman who had suffered from a hemor-
rhage for twelve years is told in considerable detail. Her ailment
was more than physical. According to Jewish religious law it rendered her impure and thus unable to take part in the community's religious observances. Culticly impure herself, she was
regarded as a source of impurity for others. Her illness thus
ostracized her and forced her to the margin of social life.

Like so many who live with physical and social handicaps,
her economic situation was disastrous. She turned to doctors for
help but soon spent all that she had without any positive effect.
Her life was rapidly becoming hopeless.

To Touch His Cloak

The fact that she approached Jesus at all speaks volumes
about the impression that he was making. The text says simply
that she had heard about him. She must have heard of his power,
but also of his goodness. She must have heard, too, of how he
reached out to the sick and the marginalized. She was clearly
aware of his great sensitivity to women.

Probably too diffident and ashamed, too conditioned to

being rejected, she did not dare to speak but was satisfied to touch his cloak. Even today people like to touch those they admire, those that are famous, those that radiate something special.

Aware of the intense spiritual drama that was taking place, Jesus turned to seek her out. A considerable crowd was thronging about and many inevitably were brushing up against him, but her touch had been different. It was a touch of faith and of enormous longing. It embodied a cry for help.

Healing Faith

Her physical healing frees her psychologically. In spite of the onlookers, she falls at the feet of Jesus and tells her story. With obvious tenderness, Jesus addresses the woman as "my daughter." It was, he tells her, her faith that healed her. He wishes her peace, shalom, a life of integrity and wholeness.

The God whose reign or kingdom Jesus preached is the God of creation. The coming of God's reign into the world is meant to heal and renew what has gone amiss. Final salvation, definitive shalom, will only come at the end of time, but a beginning is to be made here and now. This beginning implies the forgiveness of sin, but also the overcoming of sin's physical, psychological and social effects.

John Paul II in his 1988 letter on women concludes from today's gospel and similar passages that "Jesus' attitude to the women he meets in the course of his messianic service reflects the eternal plan of God.... Each woman...from the 'beginning' inherits as a woman the dignity of personhood. Jesus of Nazareth confirms this dignity, recalls it, renews it, and makes it a part of the gospel and of the redemption for which he is sent into the world."

Christ's Healing Today

Today's gospel speaks to us in two different but related ways. No matter who we are and what our condition is, Jesus remains the great healer. He has a particular love for those who in a patriarchal society find their dignity undermined. A source of life and strength for us, he is at the same time a model and pattern of how we, his followers, are to act.

Today as always women more often than men are the victims of poverty and of psychological and social marginalization. The crime whose rate is most on the increase in our cities is sexual assault. The statistics that are available about violence against women in the home point to what can only be called a national shame. Elderly women who in many cases survive many years beyond the death of their husbands often end their lives in poverty and loneliness.

The church as the body of Christ is called to continue Jesus' healing presence in the world. As individuals and as a community we need to ask how we contribute to this. The all too few institutions that attempt in our name to serve women in their differing needs require our support.

The Prophet

14TH SUNDAY IN ORDINARY TIME
Readings: Ezek 2:2–5, 2 Cor 12:7–10, Mk 6:1–6

Over the centuries many Christians have suffered from the widespread phenomenon of unbelief. Why, they ask, do people not accept the gift of faith and love that is offered them in Christ? With time we come to realize that there is a mystery of grace at work in this beyond our understanding. And yet we wonder.

This was certainly the case of the first Christians whose basic affirmation of faith was that Jesus of Nazareth was the Christ of God, the Messiah of Israel. Why, they asked, did he die on a cross? Why did so few of his compatriots recognize him? Today's gospel reflects in part at least an attempt to struggle with such questions.

The inhabitants of Jesus' hometown were astonished at his teaching and at the miracles that were worked through him. These clearly pointed to something extraordinary, to a very special presence of God in him. Their incipient faith, however, dissolved when they recalled that he was just one of them, the carpenter, the son of Mary, someone they knew.

Without Honor

Mark says that Jesus was amazed at their lack of faith. He adds that he could work no miracles there with the exception of a few cures. Faith was so central to all that Jesus stood for that without it his ministry could bear no fruit.

Jesus sums up what happened in a phrase: A prophet is only without honor, only despised, in his own town and country and among his own people. Here as elsewhere Jesus relates his experience to that of the great prophets of Jewish history, to people like Isaiah, Jeremiah and Ezekiel.

The prophets were among the most distinctive figures of the religion of Israel. Strong individuals with a real sense of vocation, they came to exercise key roles in the life of the community and through their writings and those of their disciples in subsequent Jewish and Christian history as well.

Messengers of God

The biblical prophet is not primarily someone who foretells the future, but rather someone who proclaims in the present the concrete implications of the word of God. All the great prophets believed themselves to be singled out by God for a particular task. Their accounts of their vocation experiences are among the most moving pages of the Bible. Some reacted with enthusiasm and alacrity; others, like Jeremiah, tried to escape their destiny.

Today's first reading is part of a much longer account of Ezekiel's experience. Called by God, the prophet receives the gift of the Spirit. The word that he is to preach is, initially, one of condemnation and challenge. He is to warn his contemporaries of their sins and to call them to conversion.

The message of the prophets varied considerably. Sometimes it was threatening, at other times it offered hope and consolation. The more challenging prophets were, the more they tended to be rejected and even persecuted. The fate of prophets was rarely a happy one. Jesus' own destiny will be no different.

The Rejected Prophet

What happened to Jesus in Nazareth is a foreshadowing of the rejection that will lead to the cross. Although he preached good news for everyone and especially for the "little ones" of this world, many perceived him as a threat. Provoked and scandalized, they turned against him.

The fate of Jesus has often been shared by his followers. Today's second reading reveals something of Paul's struggle to live out his apostolic and prophetic mission. He describes certain difficulties he met as a thorn in the flesh. Although it has been interpreted differently, some take the phrase to refer to opposition that he encountered both in and outside the Christian community. Whatever it is, Paul sees it and the other hardships and persecutions that he has undergone as signs that the good he does comes not from him but from Christ.

Through both ordained ministers and the laity the church is called to keep alive the prophetic voice of Christ. It is a voice that consoles and encourages but which at times must also speak out against what is evil and destructive. To defend the rights of children in the womb as well as those of the elderly and the chronically ill, to involve oneself on behalf of justice at home and in the third world, to stand up for battered women and native peoples, to reject greed and crass consumerism: such things in our culture demand a certain prophetic quality. People who do them will often meet with rejection.

Sacrament of Salvation

15TH SUNDAY IN ORDINARY TIME
Readings: Amos 7:12–15, Eph 1:3–14, Mk 6:7–13

The second reading for the Sunday liturgies for the next several weeks is taken from the letter to the Ephesians. Although scholars disagree about whether the letter was written by Paul or by one of his disciples, they are one in recognizing its unique theological vision. Among all the writings of the New Testament it offers the most developed understanding of the church and of its place in God's plan of salvation.

Today's excerpt contains the hymnic prayer or blessing with which the letter begins. It praises and thanks God for all that he has done in Christ. In recounting our motives for praising God, it points forward to the contents of the whole letter.

At the heart of Ephesians is the notion of the divine mystery. The word "mystery" here evokes much more than simply the radical incomprehensibility of God; it points to God's plan for creation, a plan that existed from the beginning but which until now has remained hidden. The great affirmation of the letter is that this plan has been revealed in Christ. He is the mystery made visible, the manifestation in human form of God's intention for the world and for humankind.

Creation and Redemption

The great heresy that threatened early Christianity is known as Gnosticism. Fed by an overwhelming sense of evil and meaninglessness, it viewed the body as sinful and history as leading nowhere. Longing for liberation from both, people sought salvation by an escape from this world. Christian Gnostics tended to reject the Old Testament and to oppose the Father of Jesus to the God of creation.

141

This kind of religious sensitivity has reappeared throughout Christian history under a variety of guises. It is sometimes met in our own day. Contemporary Gnostics, despairing of the world as hopelessly sinful, are unable to recognize it as God's creation for which in Christ we have a responsibility.

Gnostic pessimism is clearly one-sided. Catholicism has always taught a profound continuity between creation and redemption. John Paul II affirms it eloquently in the opening sentence of his first encyclical: "The redeemer of humanity, Jesus Christ, is the center of the universe and of history." A little later on in the same document, he describes redemption as "this tremendous mystery of love in which creation is renewed."

The Divine Plan

The first Christians were anything but modest in their claims about Christ. Although he had lived far from the centers of power and prestige, and although his own brief public ministry ended in rejection and death, they did not hesitate to see the fate of everything and of everyone as dependent on him. In him God, the God of creation, had entered into human life and had both revealed and brought about its salvation.

Ephesians affirms that Christ, the Word incarnate, belonged to God's plan from the beginning. Human beings as made in the divine image and likeness are called to share God's life. If sin distorted our relationship to God and undermined creation, Christ has overcome our sinfulness and renewed creation from within. In him God will one day gather up all things and through him bring them to their fulfillment.

Christ the Sacrament

The earliest Latin versions of the New Testament translated the Greek word *mysterion*, mystery, as *sacramentum*. It was thus that Christ came to be called the sacrament of God's salvation. In the human face and the human destiny of Jesus the love and mercy of God are made visible.

History did not end with the coming of Christ. In him a new stage, a new moment, began. All things will only be subjected to God in Christ at the end of time. The period between the first and second comings of Christ is the time of the church. The letter to the Colossians, which shares much of the theology of Ephesians, affirms that the mystery revealed in Christ continues in the church.

Christ and the church are inseparable. He is the head of the body which is the church. It shares in his mission. Like him, and in radical dependence on him, it is called to be a sacrament of salvation. Its task is to live out of, and to bear witness to, God's loving plan for humankind and for the whole of creation. It will only be able to do this to the degree that we, its members, accept our responsibility for one another and for the earth.

Shepherd and Guardian

16TH SUNDAY IN ORDINARY TIME
Readings: Jer 23:1–6, Eph 2:13–18, Mk 6:30–34

In spite of our urban and technological culture, the image of the shepherd still speaks to many people at a fairly profound level. There is, for example, probably no better known or better loved psalm than the one in today's liturgy, the one which begins: "The Lord is my shepherd, there is nothing I shall want."

For people in the ancient Near East, including the Israelites, the tending of flocks of sheep and goats was an everyday occurrence. The shepherd's role was cherished as crucial for the economic well-being of families and larger communities. In such a culture nothing was more natural for those who experienced the guiding and protecting presence of God in their lives than to think of him as a shepherd and of themselves as his flock.

For the people of the Bible God was not distant but near. He had not only freed them from slavery and made them a people, but he continued, like a shepherd, to lead them along the sometimes tortuous path of their history. No matter how dark the way or threatening the evil that faced them, they knew that he was there. "With your rod and your staff...you give me comfort."

Christ the Shepherd

In the New Testament the language of the shepherd is applied not to God but to Jesus. It is as if God's providential care for us is now focused on, and made visible in, the tenderness and concern of Jesus. Developed most explicitly in the parable of the good shepherd, this sense of Jesus as the shepherd of God's people is present in today's gospel.

We are told that Jesus had pity on the crowd "because they

were like sheep without a shepherd." Today's first reading offers an illuminating parallel. Through Jeremiah God condemns those leaders through whose failures the people have been defeated and driven into exile. The prophetic books are full of condemnations of priests and prophets, kings and generals, who have scandalized, misled, and abandoned their flock.

Jeremiah points to a future when God will gather his people and place over them shepherds who will truly serve them. The mention of a future king from the line of David was interpreted by Christians as a reference to Jesus. The New Testament calls Jesus "the shepherd and guardian of our souls."

Gathering the Flock

Today's second reading describes in different language the traditional hope of Israel that the messianic shepherd would gather together the scattered and demoralized flock of God. Christ, Paul affirms, is a source of unity and reconciliation. He has broken down the dividing wall of hostility that separated Jews and Gentiles.

For Jewish Christians of the first century, the great example of human division was that between Jew and Gentile. For us their enmity can stand for and symbolize the great divisions of our time, divisions based on wealth and power, sex and race, nationalism and political ideology.

Christ is the new Adam, the beginning of a new humanity, a humanity in which traditional divisions lose their significance. Reconciling us with God, he reconciles us with one another. This, in principle, is what he has done. How to translate it into everyday life, into the life of our families, our community and our world is the challenge and the test of Christian maturity.

Contemporary Shepherds

As much as the first Christians experienced the continuing presence of Christ the good shepherd among them, they took seriously the need for community leadership. Apostles and prophets, elders and overseers, were recognized as sharing in and rendering present the pastoral concern of the risen Christ.

1 Peter, for example, encourages church leaders to "tend the flock of God...not by constraint but willingly, not for shameful gain but eagerly, not as domineering over those in your charge but by being examples to the flock." To be ordained is to accept a "shepherding" responsibility within the community involving preaching and teaching and the gathering of people for prayer and the sacraments and especially for the eucharist.

The failings of priests and bishops are more serious than those of other professionals because what is at stake with them is more than a betrayal of professional trust. It involves the denial and distortion of Christ's own pastoral love for his people. To be a church leader today is by no means easy. People who accept the challenge need our encouragement and support and, most of all, our prayers.

A Gift of Bread

17TH SUNDAY IN ORDINARY TIME
Readings: 2 Kgs 4:42–44, Eph 4:1–6, Jn 6:1–15

The gospel today and for the next four Sundays is taken from John, chapter 6. This break from our more or less continuous reading of Mark will provide an opportunity to hear again the famous discourse of Jesus on the bread of life. Today's reading introduces it with an account of the multiplication of the loaves and fishes.

Containing many fewer miracle stories than the other gospels, John tends to develop them at somewhat greater length and to relate them to extended speeches of Jesus that have some connection with them. The focus of the teaching in John is not, as in the other gospels, the kingdom of God but rather Jesus himself and the gift of life and salvation that he brings.

Unlike Mark's account of the loaves and fishes, the initiative in John's version is entirely with Jesus. There is no mention of any need or of the lateness of the hour. The feeding of the crowd is a sign that in him God is present in the world offering people the food of life. The subsequent discourse will make clear that this food is the word and the person of Jesus.

The Goodness of God

Psalm 145 from which today's responsorial psalm is taken is a hymn of praise to the glory and greatness of God but also to his goodness and compassion. If his power is manifested in the beauty and vastness of the universe, his mercy is evident in his unfailing provision of food for his creatures.

Today's first reading offers an Old Testament parallel to the gospel. Like many of the miracles of Jesus the multiplication of the loaves was foreshadowed in the life of Elisha. If in his case twenty loaves were enough to feed a hundred, with Jesus five loaves will feed five thousand. The goodness of God revealed in creation and in providence has become manifest in an even more dramatic way with the appearance of Jesus.

John's account of how Jesus "took the loaves, gave thanks, and gave them to all who were sitting" clearly evokes the eucharist. Christians hearing the story of the feeding of the multitude recognize in it not just a past event but a present reality. Jesus continues to be in our midst, welcoming us to his table and feeding us with the bread of life.

One Bread, One Body

Today's text ends, as is often the case in John's accounts of miracles, with a misunderstanding. Seeing the sign, people acclaim Jesus as the prophet of the end times and want to make him king. Without waiting to argue with them, Jesus escapes into the hills. His action points ahead to his testimony before Pilate: "My kingdom is not of this world."

If Jesus did not come to establish a worldly kingdom, he did gather disciples who after his resurrection became an organized and visible community. The church exists to keep alive the memory of Jesus and to continue his mission.

The eucharist is central to the meaning and mission of the church. At it Jesus continues to gather and to nourish us. The reading from Ephesians suggests something of the attitude that we who share at his table ought to have.

One Body, One Spirit

Paul begs his readers to live a life worthy of their calling. He emphasizes compassion and understanding, forgiveness and mercy. If the church is to fulfill its mandate to be in the world a sign and sacrament of the salvation brought by Jesus, it will have to be marked by unity and love.

One of the sadder features of contemporary church life is the amount of anger and divisiveness that are a part of it. When we are tempted to add to them we could hardly do better than to listen to Paul's advice. He asks us to make every effort to foster unity and peace. Differences and tensions are inevitable. Paul does not deny them; he rather encourages us to "bear with one another charitably, in complete selflessness, gentleness and patience."

Early Christianity knew conflict and division. Sometimes they were rooted in sin, sometimes in personalities, sometimes in changing cultural situations. In spite of all divisiveness, however, Paul and the other writers of the New Testament persisted in proclaiming an ideal of unity. "There is one Lord, one faith, one baptism, one God who is Father of all." As we gather at the eucharistic table we need to remember that together we constitute a single body animated by a single Spirit. Our faith should make us patient and understanding toward one another.

Bread from Heaven

18TH SUNDAY OF ORDINARY TIME
Readings: Ex 16:2–4 , 12–16, Eph 4:17, 20–24, Jn 6:24–35

Today's gospel contains the beginning of Jesus' discourse on the bread of life. As so often in John it is marked by misunderstanding on the part of those who engage in conversation with Jesus. Their very motive in coming to him is questionable. They did not understand the "sign" that he had given them in the multiplication of the loaves. All they want is bread to eat.

The misunderstanding continues in what follows. It is almost as if the world of ordinary experience is incapable of grasping the message and gift from God that Jesus represents. In the synoptics Jesus begins by calling his hearers to conversion. In John, he leads them forward by challenging their understanding and opening up for them new and surprising horizons.

Ordinary food "cannot last." They should not, therefore, worry so much about it, but rather seek "the food that endures to eternal life." Jesus is not denying the importance of bread and money and the other things we need to survive. He is simply pointing out that they are not everything. Their significance, in fact, ends with death beyond which is life eternal. It is this kind of life that Jesus came to bring into the world.

Bread in the Wilderness

The first reading evokes a moment in the story of the Israelites' journey through the desert from Egypt to Sinai. Although freed from slavery they have not yet arrived at the land that God has promised them. The way is longer and more difficult than they had imagined. In the face of present need, the suffering endured under Pharaoh seems less onerous than it once did. They murmur against Moses and Aaron and ultimately against God.

The word "manna" was popularly thought to come from the Hebrew phrase "What is it?" Like the quail, it seems to have been a natural phenomenon, the honeylike droppings from a small tree that grows in Palestine and Sinai. Its sudden appearance in sufficient quantity to feed the people became for them a sign of God's providential care.

Today's psalm includes the story of the manna among the great deeds of God that have been handed on from generation to generation. Called "the bread of angels," it has become a symbol of God's continuing graciousness to his people.

The True Bread

Jesus' interlocutors refer to the manna as something concrete that was given them in the past and wonder what Jesus has to offer in comparison with it. It was a clear manifestation of Moses' greatness. In response, Jesus turns their attention from Moses to God and from the past to the present. Here and now the Father is offering them "the true bread," the bread that "gives life to the world." This bread, he adds, is himself.

If life as we know it requires food and drink in order to survive, let alone flourish, then the life of the spirit, eternal life, life lived in the presence of God, human life, in short, at its deepest and most authentic levels, needs a corresponding nourishment if it is to escape dissolution and death. Jesus' person and teaching have been given us by God as food and drink for our spirits. It is through faith that God's gift becomes operative in us. To come to Jesus is to believe in him.

The New Self

If faith is our first response to Jesus, today's second reading makes clear that faith in him must have an impact on our entire life. There ought to be, Paul says, a noticeable difference in the way that believers and non-believers live. He describes their life as "aimless" and as corrupted by empty desires. To believe in God, Christ, and the dignity and value of human beings is to find meaning and purpose for life.

Paul speaks of believers undergoing "a spiritual revolution" and of putting on "a new self." This is not something that happens once and for all. It begins, of course, at baptism, but it remains the task of a lifetime. It is something into which we grow through an ongoing series of small struggles and decisions. What it entails should not be hard to imagine given the stories of violence and license, of greed and infidelity, that fill the media.

Our moral and spiritual journey draws us at times into the wilderness of a secular and in many ways amoral society. We need nourishing food if we are going to have the strength to persevere on our path. Such food is available. Jesus is the true bread who in the eucharist, the scriptures, and prayer offers himself as nourishment for our souls.

To Imitate God

19TH SUNDAY IN ORDINARY TIME
Readings: 1 Kgs 19:4–8, Eph 4:30–5:2, Jn 6:41–51

Today's second reading contains a surprising invitation. "Imitate God," Paul says, as his beloved children. What this might mean becomes a little clearer when he adds, "follow Christ." The imitation of God takes on concrete form in Christian discipleship. In the life and attitudes of Jesus we see in a humanly approachable form something of what God is like.

Paul focuses in the present text on Jesus' self-giving love. The reference is to his death, but it applies just as well to his life. Jesus was the man for others, the one whose whole being was centered on his mission and ministry. In the language of today's gospel, he offered himself as bread to be consumed in order to give life to the world.

In Jesus, Paul says, God both loved us and forgave us. It is this double attitude of love and forgiveness that he invites us to imitate. The text suggests something of what it implies: rather than bearing a grudge or losing our temper, we are to forgive one another.

As Beloved Children

All this sounds, of course, very idealistic, for we live in a world where anger and violence are everyday occurrences. They mark the life of our streets and of many of our families. Public discourse in many countries today seems at times to be little more than spitefulness and the calling of names. Such things are only intensified when people are confronted by economic difficulties and doubts about their collective future.

What is true today was true when Jesus and Paul lived. People then were basically like people now, capable of good but capable also of great evil. Political and social life in the first century was in many ways far worse than our own. And yet Jesus invited his disciples to pray for their enemies, and Paul encouraged believers to be kind and forgiving with one another.

All this is as realistic or as unrealistic today as it was then. What makes it possible, Paul says, is that we are God's children. Somehow, in and through Christ and through the gift of the Spirit, we share in the very life of God. It is only by being in God and in Christ, that we are able to imitate them.

The Bread of Life

Life in all its forms is precarious and, without what nurtures and fosters it, it soon atrophies. We have to exercise our capacities whether physical, intellectual, moral, or spiritual and nourish them in ways that are appropriate. This is even more the case if we want to imitate God by following Christ.

The image of Jesus as the bread of life suggests that everything about him is meant to nourish spiritual life. His teaching and activity, for example, provide food for our minds and imaginations. They give us something to think about, an ideal on which to reflect. The history of Christian contemplation and of all that has fostered it from writings to the visual arts witnesses to how our forebears responded to this gift.

The images that dominate the contemporary electronic media are rarely religious or even all that moral. Many of the most clever of them serve commercial purposes. These are the images to which we are daily exposed. To nurture a life that goes beyond what is embodied in them, we need to feed our imaginations with other images, with the story and the teaching of the gospel.

A Fragrant Sacrifice

If Jesus is already the bread of life as the object of our faith and prayer, he is it in an even more striking way in the eucharist. The last verse of today's gospel marks a shift in the discourse on the bread of life. In it for the first time the reference is clearly to the eucharist. "The bread that I shall give is my flesh for the life of the world."

The word "give" here evokes the self-giving of Jesus that is so central to the accounts of the last supper. It is also reminiscent of today's second reading. In calling attention to the love of Christ, Paul affirms that in him the meaning of religion and sacrifice was transformed. Christ's self-giving love was the perfect sacrifice that fulfilled all religion.

The love of Jesus Christ, a love that marked his whole life including his fidelity in the face of death, constitutes true life, the life that God both is and wants to communicate to us. This is what we render present in the eucharist. To share in the eucharistic bread is to be caught up into the self-giving of Jesus. To do this consciously and in a way that spills over into daily life is to follow Christ and to imitate God.

A Gift of Wisdom

20TH SUNDAY IN ORDINARY TIME
Readings: Prov 9:1–6, Eph 5:15–20, Jn 6:51–58

The wisdom that was widely cherished in the cultures surrounding ancient Israel was above all practical wisdom. Neither philosophical nor scientific, it had to do with life, with ordinary life. The wise person knew how to live, how to make moral decisions, how to bring up a family, how to deal with pain and sickness and death. Wisdom was the pedagogue of a good life.

Israel shared this sense of wisdom and enshrined much of what was best in it in the wisdom books of the Bible. Full of proverbs and aphorisms, they offer advice on parent-child relations, the qualities of a good wife, the importance of honesty, and the need for moderation. For Israel, however, wisdom had a deeper meaning. It was a divine quality by which God had created the world and by which he continued to guide it according to his plan.

In today's first reading Lady Wisdom, a typical biblical personification of wisdom, establishes a house and invites passersby to share in a rich banquet. Only the foolish refuse. Those who come are filled with the very wisdom of God.

Wisdom Incarnate

Jesus was a teacher of wisdom. Much of what he said and the way that he said it awakened in his hearers a sense of recognition. Here was someone who spoke with the accent of ancient wisdom but who had something new to say. Divine wisdom seemed to dwell with him.

The first part of the discourse on the bread of life presents Jesus as God's wisdom in human form. To come to him, to believe in him, is to open oneself to the gift of God's wisdom. In the section contained in today's gospel the focus shifts to the eucharist. The reaction to what Jesus has to say about it is one of scandal.

The eucharist in some sense continues both the gift and the scandal of the incarnation. To believe as many do today in a spiritual dimension of life, to believe even in God, is one thing, but to believe that God is near to us, that he cares for us, that he loves us so much that in order to share his life with us he entered into and identified with a particular human being is quite another thing.

Flesh and Blood

The eucharist, like the incarnation, brings the most spiritual of realities to us in a way that speaks to our embodied existence. Nothing could be more natural than the sharing of bread and wine, nothing more ordinary than the regular celebration of a common ritual. What makes such ordinary and natural things so precious is that in and through them we encounter the life-giving presence of Jesus Christ, the wisdom of God incarnate.

Jesus insists that we eat his flesh and drink his blood. The language is deliberately provocative. Because human life as God intended it involves the body, a purely spiritual religion is not enough. Our way to God as revealed in Christ includes sacraments. These, however, are of no avail without faith. It is here that the two parts of the discourse find their unity. Faith draws us to the eucharist and is in turn nourished by it.

Redeeming the Time

In today's second reading, Paul echoes the theme of foolishness and wisdom. He exhorts his readers to be wise and not senseless in the way they lead their lives. Although the age may be a wicked one, they are to make the most of the time given them. One translation says that we are to "redeem the time." This seems to suggest that we should not waste time in lamenting what is evil in the world, but rather do something positive, and by that fact make it a little more as God intended it to be.

To the evil of the age Paul opposes the gift of the Spirit, the Spirit who beings wisdom and understanding and insight. Instead of fleeing the challenges of maturity in drugs, alcohol, and a life of sheer entertainment, we need to find a source of inner strength. For Paul, such a source is in the liturgy.

Today as always, wisdom needs to be nourished. Entertainment, a good thing within bounds, threatens in our culture to become a way of life. To try to live on it alone is to live on junk food. The spirit needs something more substantial. We need to read the scriptures, to reflect prayerfully on them, and to come together as a community of faith in order to celebrate the eucharist. As the bread of life, it offers us a share in the banquet of divine wisdom.

Choose the Lord

21ST SUNDAY IN ORDINARY TIME
Readings: Jos 24:1–2, 15–18, Eph 5:21–32, Jn 6:60–69

Today's gospel brings to a climax the discourse on the bread of life. Jesus is the messenger of God, divine wisdom incarnate, the living bread that has come down from heaven to bring salvation to the world. The way to God and to eternal life stands open to those who believe in him. If this is what Jesus is in himself, he continues to make it available to believers in a special way in the eucharist.

We are told that many of those who up to this point were followers of Jesus find what he is now saying intolerable. They cannot either themselves believe or imagine how anyone else could. And so they turn away and no longer walk with him.

In an exchange reminiscent of the scene at Caesarea Philippi in the synoptic gospels, Jesus asks the twelve whether they, too, will leave. Peter answers for them and in his answer gives us an insight into what might be called the stages of faith.

Believing in Jesus

Faith for many today is neither easy nor obvious. Our culture, as positive as it is in so many of its aspects, is not conducive to a religious view of life. It places a premium on science and technology and on a problem-solving approach to life in general. Urban living, the bureaucratic mentality, the rationalization of resources and institutions: such things emphasize our ability to manipulate and control. They leave little room for the world of mystery.

Although brought up in a Christian tradition, many of us at some point or other will pass through a crisis of faith. We will wonder if God exists and, if he does, whether he could possibly be interested in us and love us. We will wonder about Christ and about the church, so obviously prone to sin and failure in its members, including those who hold leadership positions in it.

At such times, our faith may only go as far as the first part of Peter's answer. To whom shall we go? There is nothing in the modern world, from science and consumerism to Marxism and psychology, that can offer ultimate healing and meaning. We may doubt, but that is not reason enough to turn from Christ.

Choose Christ

Faith cannot always live in a state of crisis. It will either grow or atrophy, either become mature or gradually disappear altogether. Today's first reading records a dramatic moment in the life of Israel. Having led the people into the promised land, Joshua recalls their earlier history and challenges them to renew their covenant with God. They must decide whom they wish to serve, the God of Abraham and Isaac, the God who freed them from slavery, or some other god.

So it is with us. At some point we have to decide whether or not we want to be disciples of Christ, whether or not we are willing to take his teaching and example seriously and at least attempt to live accordingly. It is only by doing so that we will ever come to believe that he has "the words of eternal life." In religion as elsewhere, conviction comes with doing.

The effort to put the gospel into practice reveals both its truth and the mystery of the person of Jesus. We believe in him as the "Holy One of God," as God's wisdom and Word, because we have first experienced the truth of his teaching.

Life-giving Spirit

As important as our decision is, and as free as we are to reject Jesus, faith is never something that we do on our own. It always involves the gift of the Spirit. Human nature, or the flesh, as the gospel puts it, in and of itself is of no avail before the ultimate mystery of life. We may have a capacity and a longing for the infinite, but we can do nothing by ourselves to fill it.

It is the Spirit, Jesus says, that gives life. This applies to the eucharist as well as to the words of the gospel. Neither the one nor the other brings life unless the Spirit that inspired them is present in our hearts. Paul echoes this teaching when he says that "the letter kills but the Spirit gives life."

The interplay of freedom and grace, of human decision and the gift of the Spirit is at the heart of all Christian life. Made in God's image, we have the capacity to choose what is good and to commit ourselves to it. Recipients of God's grace in Christ, we must exercise our freedom in committing ourselves to him. In proportion as we do so, we will come to realize that he has indeed the words of eternal life.

Unspoiled Religion

22ND SUNDAY IN ORDINARY TIME
Readings: Deut 4:1-2, 6–8, Jas 1:17–18, 21–22, 27,
Mk 7:1–8, 14–15, 21–23

The major theme running through all of today's readings is that of religion and life, of faith and morality. Although it is a distortion to attempt, as some occasionally do, to reduce biblical teaching to an ethical program, concrete moral practice is of the essence of the religion of both the New and the Old Testaments. As much as God's covenant is an act of grace, the response it demands of us includes both faith and a way of life that corresponds to God's will.

The encounter between Jesus and the Pharisees and scribes recorded in today's gospel is dramatic. They accuse the disciples of not observing the details of traditional ritual law. As sympathetic as Jesus is to such laws and to tradition in general, he seizes the opportunity to reinforce a fundamental principle of all authentic religious life. Rituals and external practices, as important as they are, are secondary; what is primary is the human heart and the attitudes and actions that flow from it.

Justice and Truth

Recognizing the hypocrisy of his critics, Jesus cites a text of Isaiah against them. They honor God with lip-service while their hearts are far from him. The phrase is a devastating one and is applicable in some degree to all of us. What God wants is an honest and contrite heart, one that knows its own weakness and that struggles to avoid what is evil and to do what is good. Without that struggle ritual is meaningless.

In the first reading Moses reminds the people of their commitment to keep God's law. If they do so, he says, the nations will marvel at their "wisdom and understanding." The law, here, is the ten commandments; what they provide is a basic moral foundation for life together. Where there is murder and violence, theft and injustice, slander and adultery, community life is undermined and individuals are consumed by mistrust and self-destructiveness.

The psalm proclaims that only those who keep the commandments, only those who refrain from harming others, who speak the truth and who act with justice are friends of God. Such people will stand firm forever.

Submit to the Word

One of the great debates of Christian history has been about the relationship between faith and works. In the course of it, people have sometimes opposed Paul's teaching on justification by faith to James' emphasis on works. The opposition has been exaggerated. If Paul insists on the gratuity of God's forgiveness in Christ, he insists equally that faith must become active through love. James, on the other hand, knows that salvation is from God in Christ.

Today's second reading says that we are not just to listen to the word but to put it into practice. Listening without doing is a form of self-deception. A famous phrase describes "unspoiled religion" as coming to the help of orphans and widows and keeping oneself uncontaminated by the world. What this means is that we are to care about the defenseless and the vulnerable no matter who they might be. We also need to maintain our own vision of life, our own standards of morality, and not simply give in to and adopt the standards of contemporary culture.

Real Love

Many of the commandments are phrased negatively: thou shalt not kill or steal or commit adultery. To be moral we have to begin by avoiding what is evil, but that is obviously only the beginning. The goal is to become just and honest, faithful and courageous, temperate and wise. Jesus sums it up in the single word, love. It is a word that we may use lightly but which if understood and lived out would make us true friends of God.

Cardinal Newman in the wonderful sermons that he preached as an Anglican at Oxford emphasized the importance of practice. He warned his hearers repeatedly against unreality and illusion. Like James and Jesus, he insisted that neither religious forms nor religious feelings finally matter. What counts is action, consistent everyday action in accordance with God's will as revealed in Christ and as discerned in conscience.

We become religious, he said, not by religious feeling or religious eloquence but "by obeying God in practice." The love that Christ asks of us is not a vague feeling of benevolence toward people in general, but something practical and specific. It "must begin by exercising itself on our friends around us, otherwise it will have no existence."

No Distinctions among People

23RD SUNDAY IN ORDINARY TIME
Readings: Is 35:4–7, Jas 2:1–5, Mk 7:31–37

The text for today's gospel once again focuses on a miracle of Jesus, this time the healing of a deaf man who has what is described as an impediment in his speech. The intent of the story is to underline the power and the goodness of Jesus. The crowd responds like a chorus in a Greek play. Their admiration is unbounded: "He has done all things well, he makes the deaf hear and the dumb speak."

The way that Mark recounts the incident evokes the passage in Isaiah contained in today's first reading. Probably written during the period when Israel was in exile, the first part of the oracle bids the people to have courage; it promises them a speedy intervention of God on their behalf. The second part, more directly related to the gospel, broadens the horizon to embrace the final and definitive coming of God at the end of time. "Then the eyes of the blind shall be opened, the ears of the deaf unsealed, and the tongues of the dumb sing for joy." The miracle of human wholeness will be matched by a transformation of the desert into a fertile land.

God Who Heals

The Jews had a very down-to-earth feeling about God and about his involvement in their lives. As both the creator of the world and the Lord of their history, he was close to them and had a hand, as it were, in all that they did and suffered. Their deeply felt sense of the nearness of God and of his concern for them is wonderfully evoked in today's psalm. There God is said to save the oppressed, feed the hungry, give sight to the blind, protect the stranger, and uphold the widow and orphan. Their God is a God who cares and who acts.

As profound as Israel's faith was, it was exposed to constant temptation. Then as now, good people suffered and died and were the victims of oppression and injustice. The book of Job offers moving testimony of the struggle of a believing Jew to reconcile his faith with the fact of suffering and evil. As long as people had no sense of a fulfillment of life beyond death, the riddle was insoluble. One way of dealing with it, however, was to think that for whatever reason God allowed evil to take place now but that in the end he would destroy it and in doing so would wipe away every pain and tear and make all things new.

Jesus and the End Times

The preaching and activity of Jesus awakened among his followers the expectation that the end times of which the prophets had spoken were at hand. His proclamation of the nearness of God's kingdom seemed to echo their affirmations about a final and complete manifestation of God's saving power. Jesus' miracles were interpreted as a foretaste of the way in which one day God would bind up all our wounds.

The experience of Jesus' resurrection only intensified the hope that the end was near. It was thought to be the beginning of the final resurrection, the bringing of all people and the world itself to fulfillment in God. Although this did not take place in the way that they had expected, Christians continued to believe that in another way it had. In Jesus God had definitively embraced our history and in doing so had revealed our final destiny. We are meant for God and for wholeness. In spite of pain and sin and death, that fulfillment is already mysteriously present among us in Christ and in his Spirit.

Living the Kingdom

Although the Bible emphasizes that God is the one who acts, who both initiates and brings to fulfillment, human beings also have their part to play. To be human, in fact, is to be called to be like God, to imitate God, to live up to the fact that we are made in the image and likeness of God. If the final kingdom has already entered into human history in Jesus, it is the responsibility of his followers to make it visible in their lives. Faith is inseparable from action; it has an inner impetus to express itself in justice and mercy and love.

Today's second reading suggests one aspect of what is entailed. Faith in Jesus, it says, is incompatible with making distinctions among classes of people. It speaks in particular of the rich and the poor. Paul, in a parallel passage, says that in Christ there is neither Jew nor Gentile, slave nor free, man nor woman. In Christ we are all radically equal, equal in dignity and destiny. To treat one another in any other way is to undermine the coming of God's kingdom. It is to distort and hide and ultimately to belie our faith.

Sharing the Cross of Jesus

24TH SUNDAY IN ORDINARY TIME
Readings: Is 50:5–9, Jas 2:14–18, Mk 8:27–35

The incidents in today's gospel come at a critical moment in Mark's account of the life and ministry of Jesus. His teaching and healing have provoked a good deal of interest. People are beginning to talk about him and to wonder who he might be. According to the disciples some are saying that he is John the Baptist or one of the prophets of old come back to life.

In response to the direct question of Jesus, who do *you* say I am, Peter answers, the Christ, the Messiah, the promised one of Israel. As self-evident as this may seem to us, it was a dramatic confession in the context of the time and marked a decisive moment in the dawning awareness on the part of the disciples of the mystery and meaning of Jesus' life.

The word "Christ" is the Greek equivalent of the Hebrew word "Messiah" and like it means "the anointed one." It was a word that the Israelites had used to denote their kings and sometimes their priests and then more and more to describe someone who would be instrumental in bringing about the "day of the Lord," the definitive coming of God's kingdom at the end of time.

A Suffering Messiah

At the time of Jesus there existed a variety of ideas about the Messiah and his role. Some of these had political and military overtones; most had a triumphal ring to them. It was widely thought that the Messiah would overthrow the powers of darkness and sin and bring about the victory of God's people.

As significant as Peter's recognition of Jesus as the Christ was, it was only a beginning. The disciples had not yet understood the distinctive way in which Jesus was to fulfill Israel's hopes. We are told that he began to teach them that he would have to suffer. In spite of a reference to the resurrection, the reaction is one of scandal.

Peter argues that this should not happen to the Messiah. Jesus' response could hardly be more severe. He calls Peter "Satan," the tempter, and says that his way of thinking is narrowly human and out of tune with God's thoughts. For all his enthusiasm for Jesus, Peter has not even begun to grasp the mysterious way in which God in Jesus is entering into the depths of human experience and redeeming it from within.

Self-denial

Jesus both underlines his own destiny and explains the meaning of true discipleship when he adds that to be his followers, we must renounce ourselves and take up the cross and follow him. There is something deeply scandalous in these words, something that goes against the human grain. We flee pain and suffering. Much of what we do in life is done in order to keep them and death at bay.

Jesus is not suggesting that we are to embrace suffering for its own sake. He is not a masochist. The fact is, however, that his own life and mission led him to the cross and to all that the cross entailed: rejection, betrayal, suffering, condemnation and execution. He did not pursue such things for their own sake but accepted them as conditions for fulfilling his ministry. His utter fidelity to the task of preaching the kingdom brought him into conflict with the powers of the world and led to the cross. He accepted it as an occasion to manifest his profound obedience to God and his great love for us.

Following Christ

To be a disciple of Jesus is to follow after him, to listen to him, to learn from him, to share his life and destiny. The cross most obviously becomes a part of our discipleship when we, too, have to face suffering and death. Here Jesus' cross can be an enormous consolation. As today's first reading and the psalm both proclaim, even in the negative things that happen to us God is with us. In them, through faith, we can be with Christ. The cross for us, as for him, leads to the resurrection.

The cross, however, is more than death and physical suffering. Jesus relates it to the theme of self-denial and, by implication, to the whole of the moral life. Today's second reading puts it eloquently. If someone is naked or hungry and I do nothing, then what good is my faith?

To be a follower of Jesus means to love my neighbor, to forgive those who hurt me, to reach out to those in need. It means to do the work of peace and not of violence, to put something into life and not just to take from it. To do such things one must learn self-discipline and self-denial. This, too, is part of taking up our cross.

Servant of All

25TH SUNDAY IN ORDINARY TIME
Readings: Wis 2:12, 17–20, Jas 3:16–4:3, Mk 9:30–37

Today's gospel underlines once again how difficult it was for the disciples to understand and accept that Jesus had to suffer and be put to death. Such a destiny seemed to be utterly incompatible with their hopes about the Messiah. His coming, they thought, would mean victory and triumph and the establishment with power of God's rule in the world. It would certainly entail the overthrow of the Roman oppressor.

The extent of the disciples' misunderstanding could hardly have been greater. At the very moment when Jesus is trying to instruct them about the paradox of a suffering Messiah, they argue among themselves about "which of them is the greatest."

Jesus sums up his view of all such concerns with the phrase: "If anyone wants to be first, he must make himself last of all and servant of all." Here is a complete reversal of values. What is important is not power and success, public recognition and prestige, but loving service. The phrase returns in a number of contexts in the gospels, and in all of them the model given of the true servant is Jesus.

A Little Child

In spite of parental love, children on the whole in antiquity were not viewed as positively as they ordinarily are today. They were perceived as immature and without power or social significance; in many ways they symbolized all those in society who were in a comparable position, the poor and the sick, widows and foreigners.

In the parallel in Matthew to today's text, Jesus points to children as embodying the attitude that one must have to enter into God's kingdom. It is an attitude of humility and openness, an attitude quite opposed to that reflected in the concerns of the disciples about their relative dignity and importance.

In Mark's account, Jesus embraces a child and challenges the disciples to do the same. They are to welcome, to receive, to reach out to children and those who in their powerlessness are like children. What Jesus offers by way of answer to the disciples' preoccupation with precedence and glory is an attitude of genuine service.

Wisdom from Above

The contrast between Jesus' teaching and destiny and the spontaneous desires and concerns of the disciples is paralleled in today's second reading. In this section of his letter, James opposes two kinds of wisdom, one that comes down from above and one that is earthly and what he calls unspiritual. The fruits of the latter are jealousy and ambition. They give rise to strife and disharmony.

The wisdom that comes down from above makes for peace; it is gentle and considerate, full of compassion and mercy. It manifests itself in good deeds and bears fruit in genuine holiness. What finally is at stake here is the human heart and the most profound impulses and instincts that govern it.

Jesus began his preaching by calling for conversion, for a change of mind and heart. The gospels show how difficult it was for even his closest disciples to undergo the process in any depth. The letter of James reveals that in the post-Easter community there were many who had not yet experienced it.

Destructive Ambition

There are many kinds of ambition. We want our children, for example, to have sufficient ambition to make something of themselves, to use their talents and capabilities to a good end. We recognize and respect people in all walks of life who are ambitious to do well whatever it is that they do. Ambition, however, especially when it is directed to power and prestige, to success and money, can easily become all-consuming.

The 1980's in many ways were marked by an enormous amount of greed and inordinate ambition. Within years the media went from extolling some of the decade's great entrepreneurs to revelling in their fall. The Greeks had a word for this kind of ambition—they called it "hubris."

The story of Macbeth is the story of an ambition so out of control as to lead to the most treasonous of murders. The language of today's second reading is not inapt to describe it. For most of us ambition may be less vaulting but it, too, can be destructive. Ambition can undermine our families and lead us to trample on those in need. Today as always, such ambition stands in utter opposition to the teaching and example of Jesus. In order to be truly first one must become the servant of all.

For and Against Jesus

26TH SUNDAY IN ORDINARY TIME
Readings: Num 11:25–29, Jas 5:1–6, Mk 9:38–48

The somewhat disparate sayings in today's gospel suggest the kind of instruction that Jesus was giving the disciples as preparation for the coming drama of the cross. Having already affirmed the need to deny oneself, to take up the cross and follow him, Jesus here spells out something of what is entailed.

The theme of self-denial is particularly evident in the last of the sayings. If a hand or foot or eye causes us to sin, we are urged to cut it off or tear it out in order to avoid ultimate spiritual destruction. As deliberately exaggerated as the language is, its meaning is clear. We must eliminate from our lives everything that stands between us and God.

What leads to sin is not the hand or the eye as such but rather what commands them: the heart and its desires. Pride and ambition, excessive sensitivity, jealousy, possessiveness, lust: such things, if unchecked, can undermine any authentic moral and spiritual life. They must be rooted out of our hearts if there is to be room in them for that gift of grace and life that is meant to bear fruit in the coming of God's kingdom.

Petty Jealousy

The disciples tell of trying to stop someone from casting out devils in Jesus' name because he was not one of them. Jesus' response underlines the pettiness of their concern. It contains, moreover, a principle that has widespread application even today. "Anyone who is not against us is for us."

Today's first reading contains a similar lesson. The Spirit of prophecy given first to Moses was then bestowed on seventy elders. Although two of them had not accompanied the others to the tent of meeting, they too began to prophesy. Joshua asks Moses to stop them. Moses' answer is a model of generosity: "If only the Lord gave his Spirit to everyone!"

Religious fundamentalists in every tradition tend to draw sharp lines between the "holy" or the "saved" and the rest of the world. In their different ways the story of Moses and the rebuke of Jesus to the disciples invite us to be open to the presence of God's grace outside of what we might think of as its ordinary channels.

To Be for Us

The mystery of God's graciousness bursts all our expectations. We encounter it, of course, in word and sacrament, in liturgy and prayer, but we also meet it in everyday life. It may come in the form of a sudden inspiration or of a word spoken at random by someone we hardly know. It often arises out of the challenges that confront us.

It can come in the example of people trying to do good, to serve others, to respond to some natural or man-made catastrophe. Such people are "for us" because they struggle against what is evil and destructive and help to build up what is good. That, too, is a part of God's kingdom.

North America is becoming religiously more pluralistic. Our large cities contain synagogues, mosques, and temples as well as churches. Here is an area in which Jesus' teaching can take on new meaning. As different as the great religious traditions are, they have much in common. All profess and try to foster in the face of growing secularism a religious and spiritual vision of life. People who share such values should reinforce one another.

Avoid Scandal

If we are to rejoice in the flourishing of spiritual values in whatever form and in the triumph of grace wherever it might be, we need also to avoid undermining the faith of the little ones among us. Jesus is severe against those who scandalize others, especially children.

Among us the sad spectacle of the abuse of young people by priests and religious continues to be played out before the courts. As painful as the process is, it is important that we learn from it. Such activity is absolutely unacceptable. It is, however, not the only form of scandal. All adults need to think about the moral and spiritual impact they have on the children and young people with whom they come in contact.

Today's second reading contains a devastating attack on the rich, not simply because they are rich but because they have gotten rich through trampling on the rights of the poor. The harshness of James' condemnation echoes the teaching of Jesus. If the gospel is good news, it also demands a conversion, a commitment to honesty and justice, to goodness and mercy. To rob it of its challenge is to undermine its power for life.

The Two Become One Body

27TH SUNDAY IN ORDINARY TIME
Readings: Gen 2:18–24, Heb 2:9–11, Mk 10:2–16

At first glance the focus of today's gospel is a narrow one. Jesus is asked about the possibility of divorce. The wording of the question reflects contemporary Jewish law according to which only the husband could divorce his wife and not she him. The practice was understood to be justified by Deuteronomy 24:1ff. If there were differences of opinion among rabbis about it, these dealt not with the possibility of divorce but with the grounds for it.

While not disputing the traditional reading of the Mosaic law, Jesus undermines its authority. Far from expressing God's original intention, he says, it represents a compromise, something allowed by God only because of the "hardness" of the human heart.

Jesus' affirmation of what God intended from the beginning contains two quotations, Genesis 1:27 and Genesis 2:24. The first is from the younger of the two creation accounts, the one in which it is affirmed that on the sixth day God created man, "in the image of God he created him, male and female he created them."

Man and Woman

The second quotation is from the other and older, more popular and more anthropomorphic version of human origins. Today's first reading is from that account and tells the story of the creation of woman and of man's joyful recognition of her as "bone of my bone, and flesh from my flesh."

Drawing the two texts together Jesus says that a man leaves father and mother and becomes one flesh, one body, with his wife, because such was God's intent from the beginning. Far from being simply an issue of the law and its interpretation, the question of divorce raises for Jesus the broader question about the meaning of marriage in God's creative plan.

Today's first reading affirms that it is not good for a human being to be alone. If our social nature fulfills itself in many ways and on many levels, its most fundamental form, according to Genesis, is the marital relationship. Finding mutual fulfillment and support in one another, woman and man are called to increase and multiply and to fill the earth.

The Meaning of Marriage

Jesus emphasizes that in a marriage a man and a woman become one body, one flesh. Here is the deeper meaning of their union, written as it were into the very fiber of human life as it was created by God. Marriage is not some more or less superficial social arrangement which people enter into or withdraw from at will. It involves the deepest possible kind of union and unity. It is something in which the very mystery of God is profoundly involved. "What God has united, humans must not divide."

The significance of Jesus' appeal to what God intended in the beginning can only really be understood in terms of the whole of his preaching and ministry. With Jesus a new moment in the history of God's relation to humanity was dawning. His coming opened up for us a new and deeper relationship with God. It also began the process of healing creation from within. Paul went so far as to speak of a new creation and to describe Jesus as the new Adam, the beginning of a new humanity.

The Example of Jesus

The first fruits of this new beginning are the gifts of the Spirit and of grace. It is only when we respond to such gifts in faith, hope and love that we can hope to live the renewed kind of life of which Jesus speaks in the Sermon on the Mount and that is implied in his ideal of marriage.

In spite of all Jesus' gifts, however, we continue to bear the burden of human history and of individual and collective sinfulness. It is not easy to be the kind of creatures that God intended us to be. Today's second reading offers in this regard both consolation and encouragement. Like us in all things but sin, Jesus truly shared our life. Although the Son of God, he, too, had to be made perfect by suffering.

Marriage is never an easy vocation, all the less so in a culture like our own where its God-given roots tend to be denied or forgotten. Like all forms and styles of life marriage, too, knows its hardships and difficulties. It demands of those involved in it discipline and maturity, commitment and generosity. Human love does not simply happen; it must be worked at and nurtured. The life and example of Jesus evoked in today's second reading is a source of hope and inspiration for couples struggling to live up to what from the beginning God intended their life together to be.

A Two-Edged Sword

28TH SUNDAY IN ORDINARY TIME
Readings: Wis 7:7–11, Heb 4:12–13, Mk 10:17–30

Today's second reading evokes briefly but powerfully one of the Bible's deepest convictions about God's relationship to human life. Far from being a blind force or power, the God of Abraham and Sarah, of Isaac and Rebekah, the God of the covenant and of the prophets is a living and dynamic, free and personal being. Made in God's image and likeness, humans have the capacity to hear God's voice and to live in his presence.

The word of God, the text says, is alive and active. Like a two-edged sword it pierces the human heart, reaching to the very marrow of our bones. It brings to light and judges our most secret thoughts and feelings. Everything about our life lies open before the eye of God.

Out of the silence and infinite darkness that surrounds us, the Bible affirms, God speaks. He speaks through human instruments like the prophets, but also in the wordless promptings of the Spirit in our hearts. God's word calls and challenges, consoles and disturbs us.

Jesus' Word

For Christians Jesus is the ultimate and definitive prophet, the one who not only speaks but is God's word. To listen in faith to what Jesus says in a passage like the one contained in today's gospel is to experience again just how piercing and challenging God's word can be.

To the man who kept the commandments but who asked what more he might do to be pleasing to God, Jesus answered: "Go and sell everything you have and give to the poor and come, follow me." We are told that the man was saddened by the invitation and refused it "for he was possessed of great wealth."

His reaction provokes Jesus to some very strong words about wealth and power. It is easier, he says, for a camel to pass through the eye of a needle than for a rich person to enter the kingdom of God. The language is paradoxical and exaggerated, but what it is suggesting is certainly clear.

The Dangers of Wealth

There is a famous saying about the corrupting effect of power. The same could be said of money. As much as both power and money can be used to good ends, they can and do, especially in great amounts, have a whole range of negative effects on those who possess them. The history of North American politics, to take an obvious example, has been repeatedly marred by corruption, much of it involving the peddling of power for money.

This, of course, is not the only kind of corruption to which such things can lead. Rich and powerful people sometimes come to think of themselves as above the law and as no longer bound by ordinary norms of conduct. They forget what finally they have in common with everyone.

On a deeper level, wealth, power and success can blind us to the truth about ourselves, to our vulnerability, for example, and limits. They can foster arrogance and an unreal sense of self-sufficiency. Such attitudes are incompatible with the religion of the New Testament. Blessed are the poor in spirit, it proclaims, blessed are those who know their brokenness and finitude and who open themselves to the gift of God's kingdom.

Who Can Be Saved?

What Jesus says about individuals may well have some application to nations and cultures. In spite of recent economic problems, North America is an enormously rich continent. The kind of life-style that most of us today take for granted was undreamt of in earlier centuries. It has created what is widely described as a consumer culture.

The effort demanded to earn money and the time involved in buying and using the goods and services it makes available, tend to fill the lives of more and more people. We have little time for anything else, certainly not for prayer or worship or even in many cases for the kind of thoughtful and loving acts traditionally associated with volunteerism.

When it comes to religion in our culture, now and in the foreseeable future, one wonders what can be done. With us, Jesus says, not much is possible, but with God everything is possible. What we need today are communities of faith, communities made up of believing and loving individuals who gather to be nurtured by God's word, to celebrate the eucharist and to encourage one another to lead a life that embodies gospel values. Such communities will be thirst-quenching and shelter-giving oases in what finally is the desert of a merely consumer culture.

A Compassionate High Priest

29TH SUNDAY IN ORDINARY TIME
Readings: Is 53:10–11, Heb 4:14–16, Mk 10:35–45

The letter to the Hebrews is one of the least known and yet theologically one of the richest documents of the New Testament. Alone of all its writings it explicitly calls Jesus a priest or more precisely the great high priest, the one who sums up and brings to its fulfillment the priestly, religious, and cultic activity of Israel and indeed of all humankind.

Hebrews is really a kind of homily, a word of encouragement, addressed to Christians who for one reason or another are tempted to abandon their faith and, perhaps, return to the practices of Judaism. They seem at any rate to have a certain nostalgia for Jewish sacrificial ritual.

The letter argues that Christianity has its own distinctive liturgy, more splendid than any other. It is a heavenly liturgy over which the risen Christ presides. Through his life and above all through the self-giving that constituted his death, Jesus offered a perfect sacrifice that brought about once and for all a reconciliation between God and humankind.

Let Us Be Confident

As much as the letter emphasizes the uniqueness of Christ's priesthood, it also insists that it has not separated him from us but somehow has brought him near. He is like us in all things but sin. Having himself been tempted, he understands our weakness and empathizes with it.

The great message of Hebrews is one of hope. Christ lives, it says, he lives for us, he intercedes with God on our behalf. We are encouraged to approach "the throne of grace," that is to say, the very person of God, with confidence. In Jesus we have an advocate, a friend at God's right hand.

In the life and teaching of Jesus, God's tenderness and love have been revealed. By the resurrection Jesus in his humanity returns to God and by doing so as it were "humanizes" God for all eternity. For us the mystery of God is and always will be inseparable from the human face of Jesus and from the love and self-giving that marked his life.

A Servant Priesthood

Jesus was not a priest in any ordinary sense of the word. He did not belong, for example, to the priestly caste in Israel, nor did he exercise a liturgical ministry in the great temple of Jerusalem. His priesthood was of a different and more personal nature. The sacrifice he offered was not of animals or of the fruit of the earth but of his very person. As Paul put it in one of his letters, Jesus loved us and gave himself for us, a perfect sacrifice to God.

In Jesus the fundamental meaning of sacrifice is both transformed and brought to its fulfillment. When in the course of human history people offered sacrifices of various things to God, what finally they were trying to offer was themselves.

Today's gospel points, although in slightly different language, to the same reality. Jesus says that he did not come to be served but to serve and to give his life as a ransom for many. There is a sense in which everything that he did was motivated by a desire to serve, to serve God, first of all, but also to serve his sisters and brothers. His service reaches its high point in the self-giving of death. He gave himself that we might live.

Imitating Jesus

Our gospel reading brings out again how difficult it was for the disciples to accept that Jesus had to suffer. Immediately after the third prediction of the passion, we find James and John pre-occupied with their own futures and asking to have key positions in the coming kingdom. Jesus tells them that the way to glory for them as for him will be through suffering and death. The other disciples hear the conversation and become jealous.

Jesus responds by contrasting the attitude of the world where people love to lord it over one another with the kind of service that should mark the community of disciples. He points to his own life as a model of what theirs should be.

The words said over the bread and the wine in the eucharist recall and render present the self-giving of Jesus. This is my body, my lifeblood given and poured out for you. Truly to share in the eucharist is to be caught up in his self-offering, in his sacrifice. It is also to share in his priesthood. The more that our lives reflect the servant existence of Jesus, the more we can be confident that in approaching the throne of God we shall find mercy and grace.

Shout with Joy

30TH SUNDAY IN ORDINARY TIME
Readings: Jer 31:7–9, Heb 5:1–6, Mk 10:46–52

Both the first reading and the psalm of today's liturgy (Ps 126) evoke a central theme of biblical religion, joy and delight in the goodness and kindness of God. Before the exile the prophetic voice in Israel was often raised in condemnation and warning. The people, having strayed from God's covenant, were acting in ways that could only lead to self-destruction. Once the disaster of defeat and exile had come upon them, however, the prophetic message changed. It offered consolation by proclaiming God's continuing fidelity and by promising that he would soon intervene on their behalf.

Jeremiah calls on his hearers to rejoice and be glad. The God who once freed their ancestors from slavery in Egypt is about to lead the exiles back to their homeland. The imagery he uses evokes the original journey of the people through the desert. Now as then, success will not depend on human achievement but on God. One can see this in the fact that those who will experience the joy of return will include the blind and the lame, women with child and women in labor. Like a loving parent God will gather his children and lead them by a smooth path to streams of water.

A God of Liberation

Israel as a people was born in the events that led to its deliverance from bondage in Egypt. Seeing in what had happened to them the hand of God, they tried to keep alive a memory of it in song and ritual and in the practice of the Mosaic law. God had revealed himself to them in the experience of their history as a God of salvation and of liberation. This they could not afford to forget.

Today's psalm shows how deeply this sense of God molded Israel's whole religious life. The memory of God's great act of deliverance filled the people with joy and gratitude. It also strengthened them in the face of present difficulties. Because God had done such marvels for their forebears in the past, they had no hesitation to cry out in trust to him now. As he had done so often in the past, so also in the future would God turn their tears into gladness and song.

Jesus Saves

Jesus once compared his public ministry to a wedding feast. It was a time for rejoicing and for happiness. The miracles that he performed were an indication that the God of liberation was again active among his people working marvels on their behalf. What they all finally pointed to, however, was the greatest marvel of all, definitive salvation to be brought about by Jesus' death and resurrection.

The God who led Israel out of Egypt and who brought those who were exiled back to their homes is the Father of Jesus Christ. He is a God of salvation and deliverance. Although what he did for us in Christ did not immediately end all evil and suffering and death, it transformed their meaning. They will all one day be swallowed up by eternal life.

Through Christ, God has reconciled the world to himself. He has forgiven sins and called people everywhere to a share in the divine life. As significant as the miracles of Jesus were for those for whom they were done, they pale in comparison to the deeper and far greater miracle of inner peace, forgiveness, and love that is the fruit of Jesus' Spirit. Here is a continuing motive for delight and for joy.

Let Me See

The story in today's gospel of the healing of the blind man points to one of the greatest gifts that Jesus has to offer, the gift of spiritual vision. A poor abandoned beggar hearing that Jesus is close at hand calls out to him. His request is as simple as it is poignant: "Master, let me see again."

Ours is not an age of faith. For the first time in the history of humanity large numbers of people declare themselves to be atheists, or at least agnostics. Although some seem to accept this situation with hardly a second thought, others suffer under it. For them even health, success and the pleasures of a consumer society are unable to compensate for the ultimate emptiness of a life reduced to this world alone.

The great challenge today for believers is to show the world that faith is possible and that its presence makes a difference in their life. We believe in God, the God of exodus and the Father of Jesus Christ, the God who redeemed us and who lovingly leads us along the paths of our history to eternal life. Here is a vision to gladden the heart.

Hear, O Israel

31ST SUNDAY IN ORDINARY TIME
Readings: Deut 6:2–6, Heb 7:23–28, Mk 12:28–34

Religious Jews, now as in the time of Jesus, recite daily a prayer, the initial verse of which is contained in today's first reading and which is also quoted by Jesus in today's gospel. "Schema Yisrael: Hear O Israel, the Lord is our God, the Lord is one." This reminder, as it were, of the reality and the presence of God is followed by an invitation to love God with all our heart and soul and strength.

The Jewish religion knows many commandments, beginning with the ten commandments, but including a variety of others, especially those related to ritual purity. The scribe in today's gospel asks Jesus which of all these commandments is the greatest, the most important, the one that takes us to the heart of what God asks of us. In citing the Schema Yisrael, Jesus appeals to what every pious Jew already knew. What God desires of us above all is that we love him with all our being.

Jesus, however, does not stop there, but adds a second commandment, quoting a text from the book of Leviticus to the effect that we are to love our neighbor as ourself. The two great loves are inseparable and mutually condition one another.

To Love God

Religion and religious practice involve many things. They offer a vision of life and a code of morality. They include laws and regulations, rituals and some kind of community experience. As important as all such things are, however, they by no means exhaust the nature of religion. They are meant finally to serve, to foster, and to give expression to our relationship with God.

The God of the Bible is a God who in freedom and love

called us into existence and who both gave us responsibility for the world and invited us to live our life in his presence and in relation to him. In spite of sin and weakness, we have what might be called a spiritual capacity, an openness for what goes beyond ourselves and this life, an openness for God.

The God whom Jesus preached is a God of love and for- giveness, a God who cares, a God who calls us into a divine inti- macy. God not only loves us but enables us to love him in return.

Love of Neighbor

What is unique in Jesus' response to the question about the first commandment is the way that he brings together love of God and love of neighbor. The first without the second is not really genuine; the second without the first misses what religion finally is all about.

For those for whom the reality of God and the importance of prayer and liturgy are self-evident, the challenge is to realize that these need to be complemented by a generous and active concern and love for others. The ten commandments talk of our responsibilities both to God and to one another. What they define negatively about the evil we are to avoid is summed up positively in the command to love our neighbor.

Many today find it difficult to relate to God, to believe in, and to pray to him. The secular nature of our culture weighs heavily on us; at times it seems to cast such a pall over life that it blots God out of our consciousness. For us, a genuine love of neighbor can become a way of rediscovering God. Truly to love another, especially someone in need, can draw us out of our- selves and in the process open us again to the mystery of God.

To Give Oneself

Today's second reading evokes again the priestly theology of the letter to the Hebrews. Unlike other priests who are obliged to offer sacrifice for themselves and the world again and again, Jesus did it once and for all. His love and obedience, his self-giv- ing to God and for us, a self-giving that marked the whole of his life as well as his death, constitute the definitive sacrifice that reconciles the world to God.

The sacrifice of Jesus was a sacrifice of love, love for God and love for us. In his love, our love becomes possible. As the first-born of many sisters and brothers, Jesus invites us to share his life and by doing so to be helped to live as he did.

Jesus praises the scribe for saying that love is far more important than holocausts and sacrifices. Translated into our experience, this means that the quality of our life is the test of our involvement in the liturgy. What we are to bring to the eucharist is our life with all its difficulties and triumphs, its struggles and failures. What we are to take away from it is the challenge and the grace to continue, in the concreteness of everyday life, to grow in love of both God and neighbor.

Appearance and Reality

32ND SUNDAY IN ORDINARY TIME
Readings: 1 Kgs 17:10–16, Heb 9:24–28, Mk 12:38–44

Today's gospel contains two provocative sayings of Jesus, one of praise and one of blame. In drawing our attention to how different appearance can be from reality, both challenge our ordinary ways of judging. People and their real motives and worth are not always what at first glance they seem to be.

The scribes of whom Jesus speaks are those who were educated in the Jewish law and in Jewish religious traditions. They were the theologians and the religious teachers of the time. Because of the distinctive nature of Jewish society, theirs was an influence that went well beyond what today would be considered the religious sphere.

What Jesus attacks in them is not their learning or their religious office, but their spiritual and moral bankruptcy. They are arrogant and vain men who use their education and status to demand recognition and deference. Even worse, they take unjust advantage of widows, persuading them by various means to hand over their property to them. Not only do they do such things, but they try to hide them by "making a show of lengthy prayer."

The Widow's Mite

The second saying is well known. Watching people put money into the treasury of the temple, Jesus comments on the gift of a poor widow. The amount that she gives is a mere pittance, practically meaningless in terms of buying power, and yet, he stresses, it is more than all the others put together have contributed. They have given from what we might call their disposable income, while she has given everything she has.

The gospels repeatedly reveal how little Jesus is impressed by appearances and how strongly he reacts to flamboyant and public displays of generosity or of religion. He invites us to pray in the secret of our rooms and to give alms in such a way that the left hand does not know what the right hand is doing. He reminds those who tend to reduce religion to a somewhat legalistic fulfillment of ritual requirements that what God wants of us is our heart. Blessed are the poor in spirit, blessed are the meek and the humble, blessed are those who love God with all their heart and their neighbor as themselves.

To Give Oneself

In spite of what one would have hoped from people whose lives were dedicated to the study of the scriptures and of the Mosaic law, some of the scribes in Jesus' time were clearly more self-seeking than self-giving. They used their position and their religion for their own self-aggrandizement.

The widow, by way of contrast, seems to have been totally unaware of herself and of her poverty. Whether the treasury to which she contributed served the temple or the needs of the poor, her gift to it symbolized a desire to serve God and others. As Jesus interprets her action, it was in no sense self-serving. It sprang from and revealed a truly generous heart.

The story of the widow's mite is a perfect introduction to what in Mark's gospel is about to follow. We are on the verge of the account of Jesus' suffering and death. Like the widow he will soon give all that he possesses, giving, in fact, himself.

An Eternal Sacrifice

There are many ways of interpreting Jesus' death. At one level he was executed by the Romans because he was perceived as a religious revolutionary. At another and deeper level, Jesus died because of fidelity to his mission. In spite of the negative reaction to his preaching, he never wavered in his commitment, not even when it became apparent that the opposition was intensifying to the point of wanting to kill him.

Perhaps the most profound way of thinking about Jesus' death is to see it as a sacrifice, a unique and perfect sacrifice that once and for all achieved final and definitive reconciliation between God and humankind. Today's second reading, as indeed the whole letter to the Hebrews, interprets Jesus' life, death and resurrection in this way.

Our text insists on the eternal and definitive character of Jesus' sacrifice. Not only has he brought about forgiveness, he remains forever in the presence of God interceding for us. The implicit challenge to us of the contrasting figures of the hypocritical scribes and the self-giving widow, is, humanly speaking, an impossible one. What gives us some hope that we can respond to it is the self-giving of Jesus and the fact that it continues to be rendered present among us in the eucharist. By communicating in his love we can learn to give of ourselves.

The End Times

33RD SUNDAY IN ORDINARY TIME
Readings: Dan 12:1–3, Heb 10:11–14, 18, Mk 13:24–32

Today's first and third readings reflect the fact that we are coming to the end of the liturgical year. The gospel text is taken from Mark's thirteenth chapter, the main content of which is a series of sayings of Jesus about the end times. There will be, he says, wars and rumors of war, natural disasters and persecutions, false prophets and false messiahs. After them will come the end with its cosmic upheaval.

The language and the imagery that Jesus uses in this context were well known among the Jews of his time. Many of them, perhaps because of the suffering and oppression they were experiencing, prayed and longed for that day of the Lord that would bring the overthrow of the power of evil and the definitive establishment of God's reign.

Jesus' preaching and ministry awakened expectations about the end of the world. The experience of his resurrection led some to believe that it was, in fact, at hand. The sense of longing and expectation that all this provoked was expressed in the early Christian prayer, "Maranatha, Come Lord Jesus come."

A Time of Hope

In spite of the suffering, confusion and distress that are to precede the end, it itself, Jesus says, will be a time of fulfillment and of joy. He speaks of himself as the Son of man coming on the clouds with great power and glory. The contrast here with his coming betrayal and death is deliberate and is meant as encouragement to the disciples in the face of it.

The same tone is struck in the first reading. The text comes at the end of a long vision of a future struggle among the great powers of the world. It will entail enormous distress for every-one, but after it will come triumph and everlasting life. Michael, the archangel, the protector of Israel, will make the just and those who will have taught others virtue to shine as the stars in the heavens.

In like manner the coming of the Son of man will be the prelude to a gathering together of God's chosen ones from the four corners of the earth. For Jesus and for his disciples, the end does not mean darkness and destruction but light and radiance and eternal life.

A Time Between

Whatever the first Christians believed about the day and the hour of the final coming of God's kingdom, Jesus himself had insisted that it was a secret hidden in the eternal plan of God. What he and the apostles preached was the reality of God's final coming and its implications for life here and now.

Subsequent generations tended to relate Jesus' sayings about the future to the death of individuals. It is at that moment that each person will encounter God and pass through judgment into eternal life. Only in our own day with its threat of nuclear war and ecological disaster are we again aware of a possible "apocalyptic" end to human history.

Jesus' teaching about the end reminds us that we cannot expect fulfillment or perfection on earth. Living in the time between Jesus' first and second comings, we are able to celebrate what has been done for us, even as we recognize that ours remains a time of trial and temptation, of suffering and death.

A Pilgrim People

In recalling the biblical image of the people of God, Vatican II reminds us that the church is a pilgrim community still very much on its way, not yet at its promised goal. The church lives in history and is subject to change and to growth and decline. Its dwelling place here below is not so much a fortress as a tent.

Today's second reading is once again from Hebrews. Central to its vision is a contrast between the heavenly temple into which Christ has entered and where he now intercedes on our behalf, and the changing and passing world in which we live. When we are overcome by our sinfulness and weakness, we need to remember what Christ has done for us and what he continues to do.

As mysterious and hidden as our own immediate futures and the future of the world may appear, we know in faith that the ultimate destiny of human life and of all of creation is to be found in God. The most fundamental affirmation of our religion is that we were made by God and that only in God will we find our fulfillment. In the human face of Jesus, God's future has already been revealed to us. It is a future of forgiveness, love and life eternal.

Christ Reigns

34TH SUNDAY IN ORDINARY TIME— CHRIST THE KING
Readings: Dan 7:13–14, Rev 1:5–8, Jn 18:33–37

At the center of Jesus' ministry was his proclamation of the nearness of God's kingdom or reign. He called people to conversion and to faith and to a way of life that would correspond to God's will and would hasten the coming of God's reign. He spoke of peace and forgiveness, of mercy and love.

Although anything but a revolutionary in the usual sense of that word, Jesus was eventually handed over to the Roman authorities as an instigator of political and social unrest. Today's gospel recounts how Pilate, as the representative of the occupying power, confronted Jesus with the question whether he was "the king of the Jews," whether, that is, he was involved in a nationalist revolt against the Empire. Jesus denied the charge saying, "My kingdom is not of this world."

If Jesus is a king, it is not in any ordinary manner. He comes, as he puts it, in order to bear witness to the truth. This way of describing his ministry is typically Johannine. Where the synoptics underline the theme of the kingdom, John speaks most often of life and of truth. Jesus comes from God and reveals to us both God's will and the meaning of our life.

God's Kingdom

There was nothing more natural for people of the ancient Near East than to think of God in terms of kingship. Kings were people of power and authority, people who in the ordinary course of things had an enormous capacity for good or evil. God to them was like a king, a powerful figure who ruled over all the world. He was the king of creation, the lord of history.

The ancient understanding of what a king should be was close to the ideal of the good shepherd, someone who was willing at all costs to guard and protect his flock. Applied to God, this evoked his gracious and caring concern for the people. God's power is an instrument of his love.

The idea of God's kingdom is inseparable from God's will. Jesus taught us to pray: "Thy kingdom come, thy will be done." God reigns not just outside of us and by power, but within our hearts and in our actions. The kingdom comes if and to the degree that we open ourselves to it and try to embody in our lives the peace, justice and love it implies.

An Eternal Kingship

Jesus proclaimed God's kingdom as both future and present. It was present in his teaching and miracles and in the way that he reached out to the poor and the marginalized. It became present with a new intensity in and through the events of Jesus' death and resurrection.

During his earthly life, Jesus' kingship took the form of service. He preached the kingdom, bore witness to God's truth and gave of himself for others. In spite of suffering, rejection and death, he remained faithful to his mission with a fidelity rooted in love. The cross proclaims a kingdom of love.

In the resurrection Jesus entered definitively into the sphere of God where he now reigns. Today's second reading describes the heavenly Christ as the firstborn from the dead, the ruler of the kings of the earth. Our first reading refers to a mysterious "son of man," a figure to whom Jesus often compared himself. In our text God confers on him a sovereignty that shall never pass away.

A Kingdom of Priests

God is presented in our second reading as the Alpha and the Omega, the beginning and the end, the one who is, who was, and who is to come. To believe in God is to believe that the world and human life have a meaning and that this meaning is rooted in God. God is the source, the ground, the origin from which all things come. He is also their goal and destiny.

Jesus bears witness to all of this and in doing so reveals that the deepest truth about God is not power but love. More than simply announcing the truth, however, Jesus also communicates the grace that enables us to embrace it and to embody it in our lives. What Jesus did once during his earthly life, he continues to do as the risen Christ. Of his kingdom there will be no end.

To be a Christian is to share in the dignity and the life of Christ. As today's second reading puts it, he has made us "a line of kings, priests to serve his God and Father." If Christ's kingship of love and justice and peace will only be fully manifested at the end of time, it struggles to become active in the world here and now through us.

Assumption, All Saints, and Immaculate Conception

Great Things for Me

AUGUST 15TH, THE ASSUMPTION OF MARY
Readings: Rev 11:19; 12:1–6, 10, 1 Cor 15:20–26, Lk 1:39–56

The gospel for the feast of the assumption emphasizes the goodness and graciousness of God. Mary's song of thanksgiving echoes and even quotes various psalms and hymns from the Hebrew scriptures and in doing so underlines the continuity that exists between God's saving action on behalf of Abraham and his descendants and what is now being brought to fulfillment through Mary.

Elizabeth proclaims Mary blessed for two reasons. The first is that she is the mother of the Lord, the mother of the one sent by God to bring about our salvation. The second, and in some ways more important reason, is that Mary believed in God and in the promise of salvation that God made to her.

What Elizabeth says here reinforces something already implied in Luke's account of the annunciation. Mary was not an unknowing and passive instrument, but rather a conscious and active collaborator in God's plan. As many theologians and saints have formulated it, she conceived Jesus in her heart before she conceived him in her womb. From first to last her role was marked by freedom and grace.

God My Savior

If Mary is unique as mother of the Lord, so is she unique in the way that his saving work touched her life. For Christian faith, all salvation comes through Jesus and especially through his death and resurrection. God was present in him, Paul says, reconciling the world to himself. The paschal mystery is a source of forgiveness and of new life.

Mary is the pattern and model of Christian faith and of discipleship. She is also the one in whom we can see most clearly the fruit of Christ's redemptive action. If Christ came to renew us and to share with us the gift of his Spirit, then he did this in a special way with Mary. By accepting her role in God's saving plan, she opened herself in a distinctive way to its transforming power.

The resurrection of Jesus has both a personal and a universal meaning. It represents the fulfillment of his own human existence in God and is the basis for and promise of our final salvation. By raising Jesus from the dead, God placed his seal of approval on all that Jesus had said and done and made of it the source of new life for us.

Christ the First-fruits

Our second reading is from the fifteenth chapter of Paul's first letter to the Corinthians. The whole chapter has to do with the theme of resurrection, with our resurrection and that of Christ. Against those who deny the possibility of resurrection for us, Paul argues that if we are not going to be raised, then Christ was not raised and if Christ was not raised then we are still in our sin.

In our passage he emphasizes that we cannot separate ourselves from Christ. He is the new Adam, the beginning of a new humanity. By entering into our life and living it to the full, Christ established with all of us a radical solidarity. He took on our destiny and transformed it from within. Death is no longer the last word.

The doctrine of the assumption of Mary affirms that through death she has been caught up in the resurrected life of Christ. As the model and pattern of all believers, she already shares in what is intended to be our own final fulfillment.

Adorned with the Sun

Today's first reading evokes a famous image from Revelation, one that over the centuries has been interpreted in various ways. Although often identified directly with Mary, the heavenly woman giving birth to the Messiah probably referred originally to both Israel and the church. In subsequent verses the same woman is said to have other children who are persecuted by the dragon.

Read in the liturgy, the text underlines the relationship between Mary and Israel and the church. Today's gospel, as the whole of Luke's infancy narrative, identifies Mary with the faith and hope of the little ones of Israel. John's account of Mary at the foot of the cross relates her in an analogous way with the church represented by the beloved disciple.

Through the assumption Mary comes to share in some way with Christ in his continuing relationship to human history and to the church. Even as she embodies the goal for which we strive, Mary remains in active and loving solidarity with us. She is a friend and advocate to whom we can turn in trust in our struggles with whatever would undermine our faith in and commitment to Christ.

Children of God

NOVEMBER 1, ALL SAINTS
Readings: Rev 7:2–4, 9–14, 1 Jn 3:1–3, Mt 5:1–12

The liturgy of All Saints invites us to celebrate and give thanks for all the holy women, men and children who have gone before us, people of the more distant past but also of our own age. These are the ones who in their lives responded to God's gifts and lived them to the best of their ability. They now enjoy eternal life with God.

Vatican II has reminded us that all Christians are called to holiness. Becoming a saint does not require martyrdom or a monastic or religious way of life or even extraordinary gifts. It is something that is open to all of us within the concrete circumstances of our lives. For most this will include marriage and the family as well as work and responsibility in the world.

The Sermon on the Mount has long been regarded as a particularly powerful summation of the ethical and spiritual teaching of Jesus. It has been said to constitute the Magna Charta of true discipleship. The beatitudes begin the Sermon and already in a few words suggest the main thrust of its ideal. Here, if anywhere, we can see what Christian holiness involves.

Theirs is the Kingdom

Various types of people or, perhaps better, various fundamental spiritual attitudes are declared blessed or happy or fortunate. Those who are so described shall enter God's kingdom, share in God's reign, find themselves filled with every grace and blessing. Although such things will come in their fullness only at the end of time, they can to some degree be experienced now.

In beginning the beatitudes with a mention of the poor in spirit, Matthew is not denying that many of Jesus' followers were literally poor, but rather emphasizing a fundamental human attitude. Poverty of spirit like meekness and gentleness suggests humility, a profound awareness of one's fragility and limits and correspondingly of one's need for God.

Jesus praises those who mourn because of the power of evil in the world and who in the face of it long and pray and work for justice and peace. They shall all be satisfied. The merciful are those who are touched and moved to love by those in need. The pure in heart respond single-mindedly, with all their being, to what they perceive to be God's call for them.

God's Love for Us

Some people have described the Sermon on the Mount as an impossible moral ideal. Who, they ask, can be so loving, so forgiving, so humble, so committed to the struggle for justice? There is some truth in this view. The attitudes praised by the beatitudes are not things that we can easily foster on our own. The attempt to do so can in fact lead to moral rigidity.

The Sermon and the beatitudes are inseparable from the whole context of Jesus' ministry and especially of his preaching of the kingdom. Because God has offered us a new beginning in Jesus, the ideal that is here presented has come within our reach. It is not something that we do, however, on our own, but rather as renewed and made whole by God's gift in Christ.

In the second reading John draws our attention to the love that God has lavished on us. It is a love that dwells in our hearts and that makes us already in this life God's children. If God asks us to be merciful and loving, committed and just, it is because he has given us a share in the life and Spirit of Jesus. Christian holiness presupposes and flows out of this gift.

Praise to Our God

Our first reading is from the book of Revelation's highly symbolic and deeply moving vision of the end times. The final act is delayed until all those who are marked with the seal of the living God are gathered before God's throne. People from every nation, race and tongue are now one in praise and worship.

The angels and elders bow down before the divine throne while those dressed in white robes cry out, "Victory to our God." Their robes have been washed in the blood of the Lamb. Through the redemptive act of Christ they received the gifts of life and grace that brought them holiness.

Although John in the second reading emphasizes that we are already children of God, he affirms that what we will be in the future will go beyond anything we can presently imagine. We will see God and in coming to know and love God, we will be like God. Anyone, he says, who has this kind of hope has to be motivated to live as a child of God even now. We must, like all the saints, try to be like Jesus. This means making our own the qualities and attitudes praised in the beatitudes.

Highly Favored

DECEMBER 8TH, THE IMMACULATE CONCEPTION
Readings: Gen 3:9–15, 20, Eph 1:3–6, 11–12, Lk 1:26–38

All of Mary's many prerogatives are rooted finally in her vocation to be the mother of Christ, the mother of the Word incarnate. Luke's account of the annunciation remains the theologically most significant of all the Marian passages in the New Testament. It reveals both God's initiative in involving Mary in the divine plan of salvation and her believing and willing cooperation with it.

The focus of today's gospel is not Mary but the child she is to bear. He is to be great and to be called the Son of the Most High. He will fulfill the messianic hopes of Israel, but in a way that goes beyond all expectations. Heir to the throne of David, his true title is Son of God.

If all this can be said of the child, then what an extraordinary gift it is to be invited to become his mother. Mary is highly favored by God and filled with God's love and grace. She has been chosen from all eternity as the one in whose womb and from whose flesh God's Son is to enter humanity. Her response indicates total acceptance: "I am the handmaid of the Lord."

The Sin of the First Parents

The coming of Jesus is a promise of salvation for everyone. He is to be a new Adam and to bring about the beginning of a renewed humanity. His struggle is to be against the power of sin, not just individual sin, but sin as it has entered into and become a part of human history. In him, in Paul's language, God will reconcile the world and make of us a new creation.

The story of the first creation is a story of God's love and goodness, but also of human failure and sin. Made in God's image and likeness, human beings had the possibility of living in peace with the earth, with one another and with God. Tragically, such was not to be their destiny. The dawning of a moral sense brought with it the challenge of using freedom responsibly. It was a challenge they failed.

Today's first reading evokes in the form of a simple story the fate of men and women at odds with God and with one another. Sin has brought shame and embarrassment and a desire to shift responsibility from oneself to another and finally to some force or power outside the human world altogether.

God Chose Us in Christ

The story of humankind's original sin concludes with a mysterious reference to a future enmity between the serpent and the woman and between their respective offspring. Almost from the beginning, Christian preachers and theologians saw in the promise that the offspring of the woman would crush the serpent a foretelling of the coming of Christ. The passage has been called a first version of the gospel.

Today's second reading pushes back our vocation in Christ into the realm of God's eternity. Before the world was made, it says, God chose us in Christ; he chose us to be his children and to share in divine life through the grace of Christ.

God's eternal choice was in no way deflected by sin. The grace and reconciliation of Christ was stronger than sin and in God's design embraced and overcame it from the beginning. If this has become a reality in Christ, it is something that we must make more and more our own by cooperating with God's will.

The Lord Is with You

The doctrine of the immaculate conception affirms the church's faith that Mary from the first instance of her conception was embraced by God's loving presence. She never had to undergo in any way the alienation from God that has been a part of human history from its outset. She was born into a world marked by sin but remained in her heart untouched by it.

For centuries Mary has been seen as a model and type of the church. Born from the side of the new Adam on the cross, the church is a community of people who consciously have accepted their call to be a reconciled and renewed humanity. What happened first and with unique intensity in Mary is meant in some way to be repeated in us. If she was the worthy mother of Jesus, we are to be his sisters and brothers.

Ephesians says that Christ died so that he might make the church holy and without blemish. What Mary always was by God's grace, the church will become at the end of time when it will be brought to its fulfillment in God. To celebrate Mary's immaculate conception is to celebrate the depths of the mercy and the love of God in her regard and the grace that has been and will be bestowed on us in Christ and through the gift of Christ's Spirit.